RECEIVED WISDOM?

RECEIVED WISDOM?

Reviewing the Role of Tradition in Christian Ethics

BERNARD HOOSE

GEOFFREY
CHAPMAN

Geoffrey Chapman
A Cassell imprint
Villiers House, 41/47 Strand, London WC2N 5JE
387 Park Avenue South, New York, NY 10016-8810

First published 1994

British Library Cataloguing-in-Publication Data
A catalogue record for this book is available from the British Library.

Library of Congress Cataloging-in-Publication Data
Applied for.

ISBN 0-225-66739-8

Typeset by Colset Private Ltd, Singapore
Printed and bound in Great Britain by
Biddles Ltd, Guildford and King's Lynn

Contents

Introduction

The editor of a book on various ethical issues once told me that among the subscribers he had recruited were two Roman Catholic scholars, one known to be quite conservative, the other more liberal. Upon learning the identity of the other scholar, the conservative ventured the opinion that the editor had found a *real* liberal, someone who was hardly a Catholic at all. The two scholars in question had never met, but each had expressed disagreement in writing with a good deal of what was contained in the published works of the other. They were participants in a debate among moral theologians that began more than a quarter of a century ago. The debate revolves around the very basic problem of how to work out what is ethically right and wrong in cases which involve conflicts of values. The two main schools of thought participating in the debate are often called deontologists – in spite of the fact that members of the school thus labelled describe their theory as neither deontological nor teleological – and proportionalists. Sometimes, however, commentators make use of the more general terms 'traditionalists' and 'revisionists'. Feelings among many of the participants in this debate run high on occasions. Some of the traditionalists feel that their revisionist colleagues are unfaithful to tradition, a tradition which they see to be so important as to be the criterion for deciding whether a particular moral theologian is really one of the faithful or 'hardly a Catholic at all'.

It is easy to understand how traditionalists in the field of Christian ethics, be they Catholic or otherwise, might feel that revisionists pay scant attention to the wisdom of the ancients and grossly exaggerate the importance of their own thoughts. On the other hand, it is equally easy to understand why some revisionists might suspect that the attraction of the false sense of security provided by traditional teachings obscures the vision and judgement of many of their more conservative colleagues. It is interesting to note, however, that several of the so-called revisionists have in recent years striven to prove that their position is well founded in tradition. It is also interesting to note that, when compared with some of the greatest luminaries of the past, most present-day traditionalists appear to be more than slightly revisionist in their thinking. Given these circumstances, one can well understand why some observers of the debate might find the whole thing rather confusing. What, then, is, or should be, the place of tradition in ethical discourse? How can we benefit from the best of that tradition? Are there, moreover, as 'traditionalists' claim, some spheres of Christian ethics in which it makes sense to talk about an unchanged and unchangeable tradition?

Where ethics are concerned, it seems to me that we show eminent good sense in setting great store on the accumulated wisdom of our forebears. To do anything less than this would surely amount to sinking into the realms of the most appalling stupidity. Problems can arise, however, if claims are made that the norms and principles inherited from previous generations are to be regarded as exceptionless and unchangeable. Such, in fact, is the case in various spheres of Christian ethics. Convinced that such a state of affairs results in an inability to deal with numerous ethical issues which face us in the world today, some moral theologians have begun calling for a more experience-based ethics. It might be objected by some more conservatively minded souls that the teachings we have inherited are already experience-based – based on the experience of previous generations. To this one could reply that those previous generations lived in a world, or worlds, which differed from ours in many ways, and that we have experiences which were not even available to them. Quite apart from this very valid point, however, the claim that inherited ethics is experience-based could be fairly described as something of an exaggeration. Much of what we have received from our forebears had its original basis, not in experience, but in strange theories, scientific ignorance and mere opinions of people who were persuasive in their rhetoric, held positions of authority, or just happened to be famous.

In spite of all this, claims are often made that certain inherited teachings form part of a constant, unchanging tradition – part of what the Church has always taught. This is perhaps especially so within Roman Catholicism, where the tradition is said to be preserved in a special way by the official teaching authority – usually referred to as the *Magisterium*. The central figure in this body is, of course, the Pope. Documents written by popes certainly tend to preserve this impression of continuity. In many of them, for example, we find that support for what is being said is provided by quotations from, or references to, statements made on the same subject by predecessors 'of beloved memory'. It is, of course, quite normal and acceptable that writers should seek support for their ideas in the writings of others. A problem exists in the case of popes only because of what has come to be called creeping infallibility, or at least the tendency to believe that the chances of a papal error occurring are so remote as to be negligible. A consequence of this is the belief that one pope cannot disagree with another.

Let us take the example of torture. In recent times, some scholars have cited the prohibition of torture as an instance of an absolute (in the sense of exceptionless) norm. Usually, when claims are made about absolute norms, the proponents of this view – especially within Catholicism – point to an unchanging tradition. No doubt, where the subject of torture is concerned, the history of the Inquisition notwithstanding, many Catholics believe that such a tradition has always been upheld by the popes, and in 1953 Pius XII probably reinforced that view, although that may not have been his intention. In October of that year, in an address to the Sixth Congress of International Penal Law, the Pope said that judicial investigation must exclude physical and psychic torture. He then quoted from a letter to the Bulgars written in the year 866 by Pope Nicholas I in which the latter said that neither divine nor human law admits beating people in order to force confessions out of them. Confessions, he said, must be voluntary, not extorted. Pius noted that it was a sad sign of the waywardness of judicial practice in the twentieth century that he should find it necessary to recall this warning. It might appear from this that a constant, unchanging teaching had persisted within Catholicism at the highest level for almost 1,100 years, and perhaps longer. Something that Pius did not say, however, was that some of his other predecessors had actively played their part in making repetitions of Nicholas's warning advisable. In 1252, for example, in his *Ad extirpanda*, Innocent IV permitted that heretics be tortured (barring amputation and death) in order that they might reveal their own wrongdoing and accuse others, as was already done with thieves and marauders.[1] In the matter of torture to obtain confessions, then, we cannot even speak of a gradually developing tradition. We simply have breaks, changes of direction, very different ethical stances: in the ninth century, the papacy opposed the practice; in the middle of the thirteenth it promoted it; and in the twentieth it spoke against it.

In certain spheres of ethics, some Christian scholars and leaders have argued themselves into corners. Three such spheres are those concerning authority, sex, and life and death issues. In view of the fact that claims about exceptionless norms and unchangeable teachings in all three spheres are made by people who have or claim to have authority, it seems appropriate to me that the first chapter of this book should be devoted to that very subject of authority. We could perhaps say that there is a certain logic to dealing with the ethics of authority before turning to the teachings of authorities on the ethics of other matters. In Chapters 1–3 I describe, question and enter into debate with so-called traditional teachings regarding the three subjects mentioned. In all three we find that claims made about the existence of constant and unchanging traditions are simply not founded in fact. A glance at history reveals clear breaks here and there with previously held opinions. We also find evidence of a struggle to remain faithful to what they claim is an unchangeable tradition on the part of people whose own beliefs regarding the subject under discussion would appear to make such a stance impossible. In all cases, moreover, we find at least a suggestion that more changes should be made now.

By way of illustration regarding this last point, let me take up once again the subject of torture. It could, perhaps, be concluded by some that, although we clearly do not have a solid tradition on which we can rely, common sense and our own moral sensitivities tell us that the positions held by Pius XII and Nicholas I are right. We might go on to say that common sense and our moral sensitivities also tell us that torture may never be employed for any purpose. Suppose, however, that experience causes us to raise questions regarding this matter. Suppose something dreadful is about to happen and that, unless we resort to torture, we cannot do anything to prevent its happening because a certain cruel person refuses to give us the information we need. Such a case was discussed by Richard McCormick a few years ago:

> If I apprehend one of two thugs on their way to execute my brother or my sister (at the time, I am not sure which one), I would apply a very effective and increasingly painful armlock to find out which, so I could warn him/her.[2]

McCormick contends that, in this case, he would not call his action torture. In most discourse, he says, the word 'torture' is used to refer to the type of pain that causes moral revulsion. 'In other words, in its most frequent usage it is a value term, already containing its own condemnation (disproportion) in the context or tone.' In the case concerning his brother or sister, however, the infliction of pain against the unjust aggressor is, in McCormick's opinion, justified.[3] There has been a fair amount of discussion in moral theology circles about other words which, it is claimed, contain their own condemnation. An example is murder, which means only unjustified killing, not all killing. To return to the subject of torture, then, the claim being made is that not all cases of inflicting pain on people in order to make them do something against their will are torture. In other words, there may be cases, McCormick's being an example, in which such infliction of pain is justified, although that may not have occurred to teachers of former times when they were dealing with the subject of torture. In short, it seems to me that in adopting such a notion, one would not be limiting oneself to the wisdom of past generations as expressed in the words of Nicholas I and Pius XII, but neither would one be discarding it. There is room for development, and we too – not only earlier generations – are capable of expressing a little wisdom now and then. Indeed, it would be irresponsible for us to neglect or refuse to do so.

Although reliance upon tradition is strongly encouraged in Roman Catholicism, it would be wrong to suggest that the tendency to be insufficiently critical of inherited ethics, at least in certain spheres, is confined to that Church. Indeed, it is by no means confined to Christianity. The unquestioning acceptance of the notion that punishment should follow crime is a good example of what I mean. This is the subject of Chapter 4. In view of the fact that the punishment of criminals – the kind of punishment chiefly dealt with here – is usually inflicted by, or on behalf of, authorities, it seems fitting that this matter too should follow the chapter on authority.

Claims about constant and unchanging teaching in this sphere are seldom made in those terms. It seems to be more or less generally accepted, however, that it has always been taught that punishment should follow crime. Few, I imagine, would claim continuity in teachings about why that should be the case, but it seems to be assumed by most people that, regardless of which 'why' is the right one, the practice is wholly justified. It could, of course, be said that Jesus does not seem to fit easily into this 'tradition' if we take into account such items as the parable of the prodigal son and sayings like 'Let him who is without sin cast the first stone' and 'Turn the other cheek'. However, it has long been 'traditional' to ignore the hard sayings of Jesus. Even if we leave these gospel passages out of the discussion and accept that there is a constant and unchanging teaching that punishment should follow crime, our own experience suggests that we should at least begin questioning the accumulated wisdom of our forebears regarding this matter. That I have attempted to do.

The subjects dealt with in the first four chapters of this book are important spheres of ethics, but there are others which could be dealt with in a similar fashion. These have been chosen, in view of the enormous interest shown in all four spheres, to provide examples of general deficiencies in our attitude to traditional teaching on matters moral. If, then, it is true that tradition is not all that it is often claimed to be, if indeed many changes have occurred in important teachings over the centuries, and if more changes are needed, how should we build on inherited ethics? How can we work out what is right and wrong in those spheres in which 'traditional' teachings are simply not enough? These and other questions we shall deal with in the final chapter.

I would like to thank a number of people who have helped me in various ways in the production of this book. First mention must go to my mother and my late father, who certainly passed on a good deal of wisdom. It may be, of course, that, upon reading this book, some readers will feel that I have not made the best use of it. At the research stage of Chapter 4 Adam Sampson of the Prison Reform Trust was very helpful. Later Michael Walsh of Heythrop College and Julie Clague of St Mary's College, Strawberry Hill, read a draft of the whole manuscript and made valuable suggestions. I also gained enormous encouragement and, I suspect, not a few ideas from discussions with Kevin Kelly, Peter Jeffery, Terry Burke and numerous other colleagues at Heythrop College, the Missionary Institute London, and in the Association of Teachers of Moral Theology.

NOTES

1. For a longer discussion see Francesco Compagnoni, 'Capital punishment and torture in the tradition of the Roman Catholic Church', *Concilium* 120 (1979), pp. 39–53.
2. Richard A. McCormick, *Notes on Moral Theology 1965 Through 1980* (Washington DC: University Press of America, 1981), p. 766.
3. Ibid.

1

Authority, Obedience
and Dissent

There are at least three common uses of the term 'authority'. The first concerns ruling, governing, being in charge, being the one who gives the orders. The second is seen in expressions like 'having authority to do something' in the sense of having permission, and the third is contained in the quite different expression 'to be an authority', where reference is made to expertise. These three meanings are not, of course, entirely unconnected, and, although in this chapter we shall be concerned, for the most part, with the first, some reference to the second will inevitably be implicit, and we shall find ourselves on occasions needing to discuss matters related to the third, not least because so much of what we have inherited from our forebears concerning authority in the governing sense is often, somewhat unquestioningly, regarded as authoritative teaching in the 'expert' sense.

An important point to note immediately is the fact that the concept of power is closely related to all three meanings. Of course, having power to influence people, power to control them in some way, or power to force them to do certain things does not necessarily involve having authority. Irresponsible journalists have power to influence. Bullies have power to control and to force. So too do rapists. Deciding whether certain people do or do not have legitimate authority can itself be a very difficult problem. Let us suppose, then, for the sake of simplicity, that we assume the authority of a particular group of people is generally recognized. They may still, on occasion, behave like irresponsible journalists, bullies or rapists. Indeed, we have all learned from history books, newspapers and various other sources that many people in positions of authority have done so in past epochs and in our own time. Contemplating such matters causes numerous ethical questions to come to mind regarding the exercise of authority. How, for instance, should authority be exercised? What are its limits? Should certain forms of authority exist? When is it right to dissent from the decisions of those in authority? When, indeed, should one dispense with authority? It is questions such as these that we shall address in the present chapter, but, of course, these questions are not new. Many of our forebears asked them many times, in many places, in varying circumstances over many centuries, and passed on their findings to us. What reasons could we have, then, for rejecting or even questioning such accumulated wisdom? Several may come to light in the course of this chapter, but one should be mentioned immediately.

The 'expertise' meaning of authority referred to above is sometimes encapsulated in the expression 'teaching authority'. Within Christianity some form of teaching authority has often been claimed by people already exercising governing authority. This has been, and still is, especially the case in Roman Catholicism. Even if this were not the case, problems could still arise if those ostensibly exercising only ruling authority in a certain society, religion or group imposed certain kinds of teaching and prohibited others. This, we all know, has happened on numerous occasions in various parts of the world. What is of special interest to us in this chapter, however, is, in a sense, more basic. It is the fact that people who have exercised ruling authority both in Church and state have also exercised a good deal of control over what has been taught for centuries *regarding the nature and ethics of authority itself.* The 'wisdom of the ancients' which has been passed on to us concerning this matter, therefore, needs to be regarded with a certain amount of suspicion.

This 'wisdom' of our forebears concerning authority is passed on in a variety of ways. A certain amount is taught formally in classrooms and through books and articles we read, but a good deal is communicated in less academic ways. Authority is experienced in the form of people who are more powerful than we are, and we learn through language and other means of communication that we should obey – although we may be told, albeit in most cases somewhat grudgingly, that disobedience could be licit in very exceptional and extremely rare circumstances. The non-linguistic ways of communicating teachings concerning authority might be described by some people merely as ways of reinforcing what is taught verbally, but that does not alter the fact that some of these non-linguistic methods are extremely powerful. I have a rather vague recollection of a mildly unpleasant episode from the days of my childhood. What I am about to describe took place in the playground of my school during a break from lessons. I imagine I was about ten years old at the time. For a reason I do not recall – perhaps I had spoken in favour of the wrong football team – I was under attack from a number of other boys. I tried to escape, but soon found myself with my back to the school wall and the 'enemy' surrounding me. Influenced somewhat by the escape techniques of heroes I had witnessed in the cinema, I put my foot against the wall, propelled myself off it and shot through the wall of figures, hitting out at one of the faces as I did so. I raced away, but, after a few seconds, looked back over my shoulder and was surprised to see that nobody was following. They were all gathered around the recipient of the punch. I do not recall whether or not I felt sorry for the boy – probably because the feeling of fear which came over me a second or two later obscured all other emotions. A teacher appeared and went over to the group. The sight of him was enough to send me into hiding behind a wall, although, even to me, this seemed like little more than a futile gesture. I knew from experience that boys found guilty of fighting rarely escaped punishment. I could, of course, have claimed that I had acted in self-defence, but I did not expect such a plea to produce any salutary results because I had the impression that teachers in general were convinced that the only way to stop pupils fighting was to punish severely all those who took part in it. Such considerations of justice as I had in mind paled into insignificance when compared with the need to stamp out violence – principally, it seemed, through the violent use of a cane. Perhaps my understanding of things did not coincide exactly with what the teachers were really up to, but, in the context of what I am about to discuss in this chapter, that does not matter. What does matter is that I and, I imagine, many of the other boys at my school, understood things that way. From our point of view, it seemed that authority, or at least school authority, could be summed up in a few words: 'Do as you are told, or else.' Whether they intended it or not, that is what was communicated to us by those who, from our point of view, were authorities on authority.

In practice, nothing dreadful happened to me on that occasion. I was not even interrogated. I do not recall why that was the case, but I imagine that the other boys had invented a story about an accident while playing. After all, they too had a vested interest in not being identified as fighters. Of course, punishment was not always administered in an automatic way. A more soft-hearted approach came to the fore now and then, but, in spite of that, the impression was deeply set that authority ruled by fear.

I am not at all sure that fear was my only reason for accepting authority. In fact, I feel sure that it was not, but it was an important consideration. In a book on the history of ethics, Alasdair MacIntyre discusses this very connection between authority and fear. Thomas Hobbes, he says, noted that authority often relies upon the sanction of force. Hobbes, however, had such a limited view of human motives that he could not provide any other explanation for the acceptance of authority than the fear of those sanctions. MacIntyre points out that if an authority were accepted merely because people feared the consequences of not accepting it or merely because they feared the sanctions which would be used against them if they did not, that authority could not function as effectively as most political authorities do function. Political institutions only have the stability they have because, most of the time, most people willingly grant obedience to their authority. People do this, he says, because they see that their own desires coincide with what the authority is safeguarding.[1]

As will be evident later, while I am willing to accept that political institutions have their stability mostly because of the obedience that is granted to their authority, I am not at all convinced that people grant that obedience only because they see that their own desires coincide with what the authority is safeguarding. However, I am willing to grant that MacIntyre's thesis has a good deal to say about how things ought to be. Moreover, I believe we can say that people willingly accept authority at least partly because they see it as necessary in human society. To say this, however, is not to deny the fact that many bodies which bear the name authority are not willingly accepted by those over whom authority is lorded. Nor is it to deny the fact that many authorities which are willingly accepted by the vast majority still use fear to strengthen their position. Throughout human history much that has been done in the name of authority has been very bad indeed, not least because of the aforementioned reliance upon fear. How, then, should authority be exercised? What should be the attitude of those in authority, and, indeed, of those over whom it is exercised? Does traditional teaching help us to give satisfactory answers to these questions? In this chapter we shall endeavour to give some answers to these and to some related questions. In the course of trying to find such answers, we shall, of course, need to take a look at some of the ways in which authority has been exercised and experienced both within the so-called secular sphere and within the confines of the Christian Church. In this way, hopefully, we shall learn from our ancestors and from continuing tradition, no doubt partly, perhaps largely, through a process of learning from mistakes.

A QUESTION OF RELATIONSHIPS

A person claiming authority, writes R. P. Wolff, claims to have the right to be obeyed. What, then, do we mean when we say that a person *has* authority? We may mean, continues Wolff, that he or she has that right, or simply that his or her claim is acknowledged and accepted by those at whom it is directed.[2] In both cases, it seems to me, we need to consider the danger of harmful attitudes and feelings concerning superiority and subordination. The first point we have to deal with, therefore, is the relationship between those exercising authority and the people who are subject to it.

Some years ago, the well-known Protestant theologian Helmut Thielicke noted the common tendency to associate the concept of authority with the notion that people who are subject to it have to surrender at least a part of their own sovereignty. His own opinion was that, if it is distinguished from sheer force, authority is present only when the person who claims to have it is on the same level as those over whom it is exercised. To illustrate his point, he cites the example of a trial judge's authority in judicial proceedings. The accused, he points out, is not in a position of total dependence upon the will of the judge. Indeed this latter acts at the behest of the larger community of law, and the accused is a partner within that community. The two parties stand under the same common law, one as its champion and the other as a real or supposed violator of it. When judges give reasons for their verdicts, they do so not merely as an explanation for the benefit of the community at large. 'There is the further purpose of addressing the accused himself to persuade him that the verdict is just, and to that extent to integrate him into that community of law which is empowered to exact retribution.' The important thing here, continues Thielicke, is the position taken by the judge towards the accused. An appeal for agreement is made to that person, who is thus addressed as the potential judge of his or her own action. In this way, the court respects the autonomy, or, if one prefers, the personal freedom or the right to self-government, of the accused. Indeed, 'his autonomy is placed on the same level as the judge's authority. Both have fundamentally the same rank under the authorizing law. The correlation of authority and autonomy here is evident.' Thielicke adds that this same phenomenon is to be observed in other persons and institutions, and goes on to say much more about both authority and autonomy. At this stage, however, I wish to underline just two points. The first is the 'ultimate equality between the one who has authority and the one who is subject to it'. The second is Thielicke's observation that, because authority 'stands in correlation with the autonomy or mature independence of those who are subject to it, it can never be a permanent authority. It is always authority for the present, valid only for the time being, so long as it is positively vindicated before the higher court.'[3]

AUTHORITY FROM THE HIGHEST COURT

If Thielicke's description of authority coincided with what has always been taught in Christian circles and with the teachings of present-day traditionalists, I imagine that this chapter could be a very slim one. Such, however, is not the case.

Serious problems can arise when the equality of the two parties is not admitted and/or when a person or group of persons claims to have authority which emanates from the highest of all courts. We could, of course, easily illustrate the former by plucking an example of a tyrannical regime from the history books or from the present situation in this world of ours. We might also bear in mind teachings concerning authority that have appeared from time to time in various parts of the world as a result of the supposed inferiority of women, of certain races and of slaves. An obvious instance of the latter, on the other hand, was the long-accepted theory of the 'divine right' of kings. According to the proponents of this theory, the right to rule was granted to sovereigns directly by God. For our purposes, the most important aspects of the theory are that the king was accountable to God alone and that non-resistance and passive obedience to the monarch were enjoined by God.

> Monarchy is pure, the sovereignty being entirely vested in the king, whose power is incapable of legal limitation. All law is a mere concession of his will, and all constitutional forms and assemblies exist entirely at his pleasure. He cannot limit or divide or alienate the sovereignty, so as in any way to pre-judice the right of his successor to its complete exercise. A mixed or limited monarchy is a contradiction in terms.

As for the subjects:

> Under any circumstances resistance to a king is a sin, and ensures damnation. Whenever the king issues a command directly contrary to God's law, God is to be obeyed rather than man, but the example of the primitive Christians is to be followed and all penalties attached to the breach of the law are to be patiently endured.[4]

Elizabeth Anscombe once discussed the hypothesis of a town taken over and run in a systematic way by a gang of bandits. She compared it with present-day England, where, she said, a minister of the Crown could not single her out and tell her what to do and what not to do merely because he would like to, using the police to back him up if she were recalcitrant. She and many others, continued Anscombe, feel quite safe from arbitrary demands in the present situation, but added that this would not be the case if gangsters were running the place. 'They [the gangsters] can decide "arbitrarily" that some individual must do or suffer what suits them.'[5] This is all quite clear, but such a comparison made a few centuries ago might have been less so. I do not think it would be difficult to find instances of European monarchs in bygone days behaving like Anscombe's gangsters. A major difference between the two parties, however, is that the gangsters would not have been protected by a widely accepted divine right of kings. The very existence of such a theory and the fact that it was widely accepted and applied for a very long period is a witness to the danger of allowing authority to dictate what should be taught regarding the nature and ethics of authority. Of course, the very idea of 'allowing authority' to do anything may seem strange to some people, because they are accustomed to the notion that only those in authority can allow things or actions. That is a point to which we shall need to return a little later.

Although the theory we have just discussed fell into disrepute a long time ago, it would be wrong to say that nobody now claims to have authority that emanates from the highest of all courts. It would also be wrong to say that nobody in a position of authority today tries to dictate what should be taught regarding the nature of that authority and the rights and wrongs of obeying it. Perhaps the most obvious example that illustrates the truth of both of these statements is that of the papacy. In Roman Catholicism, the claim is made that the Pope exercises both a jurisdictional and a teaching authority. To most people's ways of thinking, the claim is an extraordinary one, for the Pope is said to have the ability, under certain conditions, to speak infallibly on matters concerning faith and morals. In practice, however, the claimed power to speak infallibly is so rarely invoked that it has played a much smaller part than many might expect to be the case in recent debate concerning papal authority.

In spite of that, claims made by some traditionalist Catholic scholars concerning what we might call the more ordinary papal authority (and, as we shall see, the authority of other bishops) would still cause many an eyebrow to be raised. For instance, regarding teachings on moral matters, Germain Grisez, a well-respected figure in traditionalist Catholic circles, admits that there are limits to the trust that we can place in a merely human guide and that we would be acting irresponsibly if we went beyond those limits. However, 'we believe that our Lord teaches in and through the Church and gives us the word of the Father. Hence, our submission to the Church's teaching is not submission to mere human opinions, but to the very word of God.'[6]

Usually the expression 'the Church's teaching' is used in Catholic circles to mean the teachings of the Pope when he speaks officially either alone or together with the other bishops of the Catholic Church. This might seem an unsatisfactory state of affairs to Catholics who believe that papal teachings on certain subjects are erroneous. Moreover, all would agree that such errors have occurred in the past. Grisez, however, goes on to discuss the assent which he believes should be given to the possibly erroneous teachings of bishops, 'including the pope'. Even when it is not clear to us, he says, that a particular teaching of the Pope or of another bishop is proposed infallibly, we have good reason for assuming that this teaching does pertain to divine revelation, the good reason being the divinely given office (of pope or bishop, evidently) and the grace which accompanies that office.

One who makes the act of human faith – that is, accepts teaching with religious assent even when it is not recognizable as infallibly proposed – can proceed with confidence and a clear conscience. If the teaching should turn out to be in error, one has nevertheless followed the guidance which God has seen fit to provide.

Grisez goes on to say that a faithful Catholic is not in a position to think that a moral norm proposed by the ordinary teaching authority is false unless there is a superior source which requires that he or she should indeed conclude that the norm is false. As examples of such sources he cites Scripture, defined doctrine, and teachings which have been proposed infallibly by the official teaching authority (or *Magisterium*, as it is often called). It is possible, he admits, that a number of bishops could become convinced of an erroneous doctrine and propose it as certain. If that were to happen, the faithful could look to Rome for clarification. 'In the case of papal teaching, however, there is little chance of its being undercut by a superior theological source.'[7] Little chance there may be, but popes have been known to make mistakes. Grisez accepts this, but is of the opinion that it was right for Catholics of the time, including theologians, to trust the judgement of the *Magisterium*. Furthermore, if instances of error were to occur again, he says, it would be impossible to recognize them as such with the clarity of hindsight that we can apply to past cases. In accepting such teaching, a Catholic might be giving assent to a false norm, but God has not provided a better one.

In the very recently published second volume of the work referred to, Grisez writes:

> Teachings which otherwise would call for religious assent can, however, be known to be in error. The responsibility to give religious assent therefore is limited, and its limits vary with the diverse ways in which papal and episcopal teachings, although proposed as certainly true, can be mistaken. Needless to say, the existence of these limits in no way justifies

radical theological dissent from the Church's constant and most firm moral teaching.[8]

Surely a situation could arise in which knowledge that a teaching is wrong is not common knowledge. Surely it could be the case that only a small group of people know that the teaching is wrong. Perhaps Grisez would agree with that, but, if that is the case, it seems to me that his previously stated claims need to be modified. If they are not modified, serious problems arise concerning, among other matters, the autonomy of those who are expected to bow to the authority of the *Magisterium*. Is that autonomy taken into account at all in Grisez's scheme of things? Is it respected? I suspect that Grisez would respond in the affirmative to both questions because, in his opinion, 'Responsibly following the possibly erroneous judgment of the *Magisterium* is the same as responsibly following one's sincere conscience in other cases; it is possible to go wrong in this way, but one has no better norm than one's best judgment'.[9]

Evidently, a great deal is taken for granted by Grisez, not the least being a very wide-ranging divine right of popes, but is he seriously claiming that one's best judgement must necessarily coincide with that of the Pope? The answer would seem to be that there is a theoretical possibility that it will not (when a papal teaching is *known* to be mistaken, or when a more authoritative teaching exists), but that the chances of such being the case are almost negligible. One would indeed hope that serious errors on the part of popes were rare, but regarding the possibility as almost negligible or just extremely unlikely would seem to me to be going too far. Many students of the history of such matters as slavery, religious liberty, torture and capital punishment would, no doubt, be inclined to agree. At one point Grisez makes specific mention of a particularly disturbing papal error. Leo X, he notes, condemned Martin Luther's proposition that burning heretics at the stake was against the will of God.[10] Surely it is incredible to claim that nobody could have had a better judgement than Leo on that matter before a later pope received enlightenment directly from God or otherwise. On the same page on which he refers to this case Grisez notes that the practice of burning heretics was clearly excluded by the Second Vatican Council. I imagine, however, that many an individual had come to exclude it long before the announcement of any such conciliar exclusion. Indeed, I would say it is very likely that, even if Luther himself is left out of the discussion, there were many people, both Catholic and Protestant, in fifteenth-century Europe whose 'best judgement' regarding the burning of heretics was far superior to that of Leo X. Such people would have needed to do violence to their own consciences in order to accept papal teaching on the matter. They would have had to surrender their own autonomy.

When I made this last point in an article published in the *Heythrop Journal*, Robert P. George responded by saying, among other things, that, in the book to which I have referred, Grisez discusses the limits of a Catholic's obligation to give religious assent to the teachings of the non-infallible *Magisterium*. Grisez's conclusion, says George, is 'that faithful Catholics can judge that a moral norm currently proposed by the ordinary magisterium is false if they are confident that there exists a superior source . . . which requires this conclusion'. As for Leo X's condemnation of Luther's position regarding the burning of heretics, the upshot of Grisez's analysis, continues George, is that a Catholic of that time, 'who was persuaded by scriptural arguments (such as those later advanced by the Second Vatican Council in chapter two of *Dignitatis Humanae*) that burning heretics is wrong should have refused to burn heretics and, indeed, should have done whatever was possible and appropriate to resist the practice'.[11]

I have already made mention of the fact that Grisez does indeed discuss the possibility of doubting a norm proposed by the *Magisterium* if a superior source exists. I have also noted his assertion that, where papal teaching is concerned, the normal grounds for religious assent are unlikely to be undercut by a superior source. As for resorting to Scripture as a superior source, much of what follows in this chapter and elsewhere in this book should suffice to show that, alone, such a procedure can be a very dangerous one. Grisez himself writes:

> Of course, only the propositions asserted by the sacred writers are certainly true, and so careful interpretation of the Gospels is necessary (see DV 11–12). For this reason one cannot ignore the work of Scripture scholars. At the same time, one must be careful in selecting the scholars one will believe.[12]

The fact that the *Magisterium* itself has at times tried to exert control over the interpretation of Scripture could lead us to a terrible circularity here.

A related though less violent issue is that of the control of Catholic scholars by popes and their delegates in more recent times. It is generally agreed today, writes Grisez, that there were many errors in decrees concerning Scripture issued by the Pontifical Biblical Commission between 1905 and 1915. However, he goes on to say, in 1907 Pius X issued a document in which he declared the force of the Commission's decrees. A careful reading of that document

> shows that these decrees primarily were disciplinary in character. Their ultimate purpose was to protect the faith, but their immediate object was to regulate the work and teaching of scholars. They bound consciences to obedience, but it does not seem they had in general to be accepted as certainly true.[13]

That is an interesting collection of assertions which becomes even more interesting when one examines the case of Fr Henry Poels, a professor at the Catholic University of America during the period under discussion. He was also a consultor to the aforementioned Pontifical Biblical Commission. It should be added, however, that the members who issued decisions were cardinals. One of these decisions, issued in 1906, was that scholars should accept that Moses was 'substantially' the author of the first five books of the Bible. I imagine that if any Catholic biblical scholar made such an assertion today, he or she would be assumed by colleagues to be joking, ill, over-tired or drunk. Such was not the case, it would seem, with Pope Pius X and the members of his Pontifical Biblical Commission. In 1907 Fr Poels told the Pope that he had scholarly difficulties with this decision. During the course of the next few years, various misunderstandings, misrepresentations, accusations and other interesting elements combined to form what, in the words of Gerald P. Fogarty, 'was as complicated as a bad script for a soap opera'. Eventually Fr Poels lost his job, but, before matters reached such a peak, he was called upon to swear an oath which read: 'I, Henry Poels, do promise, vow and swear upon God's holy Gospels that I will sincerely accept and faithfully teach all the doctrines and conclusions that the Pontifical Commission has promulgated up to now or will promulgate in the future.' Poels had a meeting with the Vatican Secretary of State, Cardinal Raffaele Merry del Val, and asked him if the words 'sincerely accept and faithfully teach' could be construed as meaning that he attributed to all the past and future decisions of the Biblical Commission 'all the authority that Catholic theology teaches to be due to the decisions issued by this high ecclesiastical tribunal'. The Cardinal did not find this acceptable, and removed all chances of ambiguity by demanding that Poels should swear a solemn affirmation of his belief – in conscience – that Moses was the author of the books in question. As one would expect, Poels replied that what was being demanded was a violation of his conscience.[14]

It is, of course, generally accepted in Christian circles that the Holy Spirit lives in the Church, that he/she lives, indeed,

in the very personalities of all the faithful. Some people, therefore, find it odd that a claim should be made that bishops, and
most especially the Bishop of Rome, have a kind of 'hotline'
to the Holy Spirit. Ever since the declaration of papal infallibility at the First Vatican Council in 1870, there has been,
even (and perhaps principally) within the ranks of Roman
Catholicism itself, an enormous amount of debate about the
limits of the *Magisterium*'s power and authority. Numerous
scholars have argued in favour of what we might call the official
position (sometimes less reverently referred to as the party line),
and some have even made claims which outstrip those of the
1870 definition. Others, while striving to remain within the
boundaries of the definition, have tried to show the limits of
infallibility, especially in the moral sphere. Finally, there is
another category composed of an apparently growing number
of theologians who, at least in private conversation, cast doubt
upon the validity of the entire claim.

It could be said, of course, that there is no question of
a 'hotline'. Instead there is merely a conviction that Jesus
entrusted all ecclesiastical authority to the apostles and their
successors, and that the bishops are those successors. Clearly,
a large percentage of Christians, notably, but not exclusively,
in Protestant circles, do not accept any of this. Even if they
did, however, the mere fact of being in charge would not
suffice to guarantee infallibility. One would still need access to
special powers. It might be claimed that this is really no big
issue because infallible powers – real or otherwise – are rarely
invoked. That is undoubtedly true, but there are those, in
Vatican circles and elsewhere, who present arguments similar
to those of Grisez that urge Catholics to treat the statements of
the *Magisterium* almost as if they were infallible. Indeed, the
urging to follow the teachings of the *Magisterium* is often presented in such a way as to remove all significance from that
word 'almost'. In short, special powers, it seems, are claimed
for those who receive the fullness of the priesthood in episcopal

ordination and, more especially, for those elected to the papacy. However, even within the ranks of Roman Catholicism, there are those who express doubts regarding the very existence of the ministerial priesthood. Peter Harvey argues, for instance, that no basis for a special priestly caste is to be found in the New Testament. Indeed, 'In Hebrews the priesthood of Jesus makes any other priesthood redundant, while in Revelation everybody is a priest because of Jesus'. Harvey poses the question why a wholesale regression from the freedom from priestcraft occurred. What were, and, indeed, still are, the needs, interests or purposes served by it? The best answer which has come his way so far 'is that ordained priesthood within Christianity is a concession to our paganism'. The entry of priesthood upon the scene manifested the incompleteness of the Church's conversion. 'Something indomitably pagan seems to have declared itself symptomatically in this way.' I should add at this point that Harvey does not use the term 'pagan' in a defamatory way, but rather as meaning simply sub-Christian or not-quite-Christian.

> It is neither shocking nor surprising that pagan elements still hold some sway in the supposedly Christianised psyche. In particular there seems to be a deep compulsion to set apart a class of people upon whom we can project an image of the mediation of divine power. It could even be argued that the thesis of Hebrews and of Revelation was premature, or that it never in practice was obtained. It is very unsettling to live in the free play of the Spirit.[15]

Undoubtedly, many members of several Christian denominations would disagree with Harvey, but the fact remains that, whatever one's convictions may be regarding the validity of a Christian ministerial priesthood, it is difficult to relate the present caste systems to the Jesus of the Gospels. Bearing that in mind, it is clear that there is evidently a need for further study and discussion about the basis of any claims regarding ecclesiastical authority coming directly from God and settling, so to speak, upon the highest members of the highest caste. Here I merely wish to note the difficulties without entering into further discussion which might deflect us away from our main subject. There are problems concerning ecclesiastical authority which arise even when no special claims are made about divine rights or divine appointments, and many of those problems would seem to stem from attitudes which we try to justify by pushing too far some of the similes used by Jesus. Adult humans are simply not children, and they are certainly not sheep. Interestingly, Harvey goes on to point out that even Protestants who claim to have no priests are not so different, for they have ministers. Thus, it seems to him that 'the free churches are no freer than the rest of us of the compulsion to envisage church life as dependent upon, and revolving around, the full-time professional set-apart God-person'.[16] It seems to me that, in most branches of Christianity, we can so easily slip into situations in which the 'shepherds' take most, perhaps all, of the responsibility, while everybody else plays 'follow my leader' like easily led woolly animals. In most cases, I fear, the fault is on both sides. So much for a healthy relationship between authority and autonomy.

> One assault to wholeness, one invitation to codependence is the term 'lay' Christian. In law or medicine, the term 'lay' means the uninformed and incapable. In an active community of believers, it is out of place: there are many gifts, but the same Spirit. The focus of the word 'lay' is on a perceived lack, instead of what gifts we do have.[17]

Interestingly, Michael H. Crosby defines 'patriarchal clericalism metaphorically as the specific addiction to authority that can be found in contemporary institutional Catholicism'.[18] He is not alone in seeing authority as an addiction in the Roman

Catholic Church. The fact that Catholic writers have specifically addressed this subject, however, should not distract us
from seeing the same basic problem, albeit under somewhat
different guises, in other branches of Christianity and, indeed,
throughout society. This is an extremely important issue and
one that we ignore to the detriment of personal growth. It is
linked to that all too common tendency to rely on others to give
us identity, a tendency confronted by Harvey in a short commentary on Jesus' declaration that anyone who goes to him
without hating father, mother, wife, children, etc., cannot be
his disciple. Versions of ourselves are projected on to us through
familial and other relationships. In order not to be trapped in
such second-hand versions of ourselves, says Harvey, we may
even have to hate. He is not suggesting that hatred is a good
thing which, in a sense, is equivalent to the commendation to
love. What he is saying is that it may be necessary to pass
through hatred on our way to mature love. 'Hatred is a sign
of involvement, but frustrated involvement. It is love unable to
find consummation. Jesus is not, then, commending some life-
denying form of holiness but the single-minded pursuit of the
task of becoming my true self.'[19] If some authority or other is
one of those 'family' members that separates me from myself,
then surely I must free myself from its shackles. Such freedom
does not inevitably lead to separation. Instead, it makes real
relationships possible.

A somewhat different kind of authority from that just discussed, but, at the same time, one that is linked to the highest
court, has been appealed to many times in the history of Christianity. Some years ago David Brion Davis wrote a rather
lengthy study of slavery in the late eighteenth and early nineteenth centuries, and included some details about what he called
'the biblical war'. One of the participants in this 'war' or debate
about biblical justification of slavery was an Anglican missionary called Thomas Thompson. For our purposes, Thompson's
approach to the subject is most interesting. Today we might

imagine that anybody who attempted to justify the African slave trade would feel the need to show, if it were possible to do so, that it was a virtuous enterprise or that it did not involve abuse. Thompson, we are told, disclaimed any such need. Instead he turned to Scripture for guidance about whether or not such activity constituted a violation of God's law. In Leviticus 25:39–55 he read that God had informed Moses that Hebrew servants should not be treated oppressively and should be freed every fiftieth year. He also read, however, that the Israelites could purchase as slaves the children of aliens who were resident among them, as well as members of the families of those aliens if they were born on the soil of the Israelites and lived with them. They were to be their possession, and could be passed on to other generations as a legacy. As Thompson saw it, a practice which had such clear divine sanction could not be against the natural law. He also went on to point out that St Paul had sent the fugitive Onesimus back to his master. It appeared, therefore, that, although Christian conversion changed the spiritual condition of a slave, it did not change his or her legal obligation.

Davis notes that, although such biblical arguments were relatively rare, they were a cause of some embarrassment to abolitionist writers who took Scripture seriously. Moreover, in 1768, he writes, Dr Daniel Burton informed Anthony Benezet 'that the Society for the Propagation of the Gospel could not condemn slaveholding as unlawful "finding the contrary very plainly implied in the precepts, given by the Apostles both to masters and servants; which last, were then, for the most part, slaves"'. A little further on Davis refers to a pamphlet written by one Raymond Harris – who was apparently a suspended Jesuit priest and whose real name was Raymondo Hormaza:

For Harris, speaking to a Protestant audience, the Bible was the only possible guide. Tradition, habits, 'mere human

reason and sense' – all were fallible. Anyone 'with any pretensions to Religion' must immediately assent to the final
authority of Scripture. And any person who professed to
acknowledge the Bible as the unerring Word of God must
assent to every Scriptural decision, without reserve and
without questioning God's hidden justice.

Having boxed his readers within this framework of orthodox Protestant assumptions, Harris proceeded to show that
slavery had been positively sanctioned by God during the
period of natural law, in the time of Abraham and Joseph;
during the period of Mosaic law; and during the earliest
Christian dispensation.[20]

At this point it is useful to say a word or two about the
'expertise' meaning of authority. In this regard Joseph Raz says
that having authority can mean 'being an expert who can vouch
for the reliability of information, or for the authenticity of
a text'.[21] This, of course, involves going beyond the notion
of regarding a particular book or collection of books as an
authority in itself, and is especially important when, as is the
case with the Bible, we do not have the original manuscripts,
there are variants in the manuscripts we do possess, and the
various documents that have come down to us were written in
ancient languages over a very long period of time and in cultural
settings quite different from our own. Thus we need expertise
in the spheres of translation and interpretation. The expert
needs to establish what was being communicated at the time of
writing and/or speaking, and what significance a particular text
has for readers today. During the last century or so enormous
advances have been made in the sphere of biblical scholarship.
While these advances have led to a good deal of general agreement being reached by Christian scholars regarding certain
matters, they have also opened the door to the possibility of
various interpretations regarding others, a possibility which, of
course, existed before these advances in scholarship were made,

but which was, to some extent, controlled. As Robin Gill points out, biblically based Christian ethics could be expected to prosper as long as a unitary view of the Bible could be upheld or enforced. It was possible for some time for such a situation to prevail because of the special status given to the biblical interpretation of key figures, two of the best known in Protestant circles, of course, being Luther and Calvin. There were some ambiguities and other problems, but these could be kept to a minimum. 'Hermeneutics is not a problem as long as one is oblivious to the crucial role of a canonised interpreter. Luther wrote this or that . . . but he was merely mediating Scripture, not reflecting the circumstances of sixteenth-century middle Europe. He was a pure convector.' Of course, as Gill goes on to say, that was simply not the case.[22]

So far in our discussion of biblical authority we have concentrated, for the most part, on Protestantism. At least as a kind of parenthesis, it might be useful to add a word or two about the Bible and the Roman Catholic Church, where the authority of Scripture meets the authority of the *Magisterium*. In recent decades a fairly liberal attitude towards biblical scholarship has been developing within Roman Catholicism, even in official circles. Earlier this century, however, a very different situation prevailed. In 1902 Pope Leo XIII established the Pontifical Biblical Commission, to which we referred above. We have already seen what this Commission had to say about the authorship of the first five books of the Bible. An article in *The New Catholic Dictionary*, published in 1929, lists some of its other teachings:

> The first three chapters of *Genesis* were declared to be literally historical to the exclusion of all fables or legends . . . The arguments used by critics to show that Isaias could not have written the whole of his book are declared to be unconvincing . . . [T]he first three Gospels were written in the following order: *Aramaic St Matthew* (the Greek translation

being substantially the same as the original), *St Mark*, *St Luke*; this arrangement excludes the 'Two Document Theory' advocated by most non-Catholic critics as a solution of the Synoptic problems; under these restrictions the Synoptic problem [*sic*] is left open to discussion. The writings of the Apostles are not to be construed in such a way as to support the opinion that they looked upon the Second Coming of Christ as imminent.[23]

I need hardly add that no Catholic biblical scholar whom this author has ever met would be entirely in agreement with all of the teachings just listed. Admittedly, the findings of the Pontifical Biblical Commission were not declared to be *de fide*, but we have already had reason to note what happened to Henry Poels when he disagreed with one such finding. It is worth noting that, in such cases, the Catholic *Magisterium* takes on two of the meanings of authority: the expert (who, where Scripture is concerned, interprets, establishes the meaning of a text, etc.) and the ruler who demands obedience.

Now let us return to the problems which arise from a tendency in so-called traditional Protestantism to regard Scripture as the ultimate (even sole) authority in the ethical sphere. Clearly, we must take care not to adopt what we might somewhat appropriately call a slavish attitude towards particular texts in the Bible. On the very question of the authority of Scripture a distinguished Protestant scholar of our own days has stated that 'Scripture *alone* is never the final court of appeal for Christian ethics. Its understanding of God and his purposes, of man's condition and needs, of precepts, events, human relationships, however, do [*sic*] provide the basic *orientation* toward particular judgments.' Within that orientation, he continues, there is room for argumentation. Scripture deeply informs our judgements, but does not by itself determine what those judgements ought to be. 'That determination is done by persons and communities as finite moral agents responsible to God.'[24]

Many, however, stick to what might be called a more 'traditional' approach. Thus, in the debate about the morality of homosexual acts, we see the Bible being appealed to in much the same way that it was appealed to during the debate about slavery.

At this point, it would seem wise to say a few words about the traditional tendency to lay great emphasis on the need for obedience and little on the dangers of such activity.

OBEDIENCE AND DISSENT

(a) Obedience

One of the most glaring examples of irresponsible obedience is that of military personnel who blindly comply with orders to do what is obviously morally wrong. Countless atrocities have occurred over the centuries because many of those who have joined the armed services in various countries have obeyed appalling commands. Moreover, 'I was merely obeying orders' has often been the 'excusing' plea of those in the ranks. In recent times, however, that plea has been rejected on numerous occasions even in courts of law. At a fairly recent trial in Germany, for example, a man who had been an East German border guard was found guilty of manslaughter. His crime was that, in 1989, he had, in compliance with orders given to border guards, shot and killed a man who was trying to flee to West Berlin. He was sentenced to three and a half years imprisonment – 'specifically, the trial judge said, for following the laws of his country rather than asserting his conscience'.[25] The verdict has caused a certain amount of controversy. It has been pointed out, for instance, that 'The idea that a legal act can be made a crime retrospectively is alien to the laws of many countries'.[26] Nevertheless, no such controversy changes the fact that it is morally wrong to shoot innocent people in such circumstances, even though an order has been given.

Mentioning the notion of unethical obedience brings to mind a whole host of other instances. The pages of our history books are littered with descriptions of unjust wars and of unjust actions committed during wars that may or may not have been just, and, of course, wars take place because people obey orders. Unethical obedience, however, is not confined to members of the armed services. In the world of commerce and in the world of the mass media, doing what the boss tells one to do can foreseeably result in the exploitation of other people, in the corruption of young people, and in incitement to violence. Enormous problems can and do occur in all walks of life, it would seem, as a direct result of obedience. Indeed, it would seem impossible to say which has caused the greater amount of damage throughout human history, dissent or obedience.

There is certainly evidence which suggests that most humans resort to obedience far too easily. As Stanley Milgram put it, 'A substantial proportion of people do what they are told to do, irrespective of the content of the act and without limitations of conscience, so long as they perceive that the command comes from a legitimate authority'. Some much-publicized experimentation conducted by Milgram himself is a significant indicator of this phenomenon. For the purposes of the experiment a number of volunteers were recruited, and each was asked to take on the role of teacher. Another 'volunteer' was to take on the role of learner and was given the task of learning lists of word pairs. The learner was strapped to a chair. Whenever he made an error the 'teacher' was to administer an electric shock, and the intensity of the shock was to increase with each error. Unknown to the 'teacher', the 'learner' was a collaborator of the experimenter. He received no electric shocks, and merely acted the part – presumably moaning, screaming, protesting and falling silent as occasion demanded. Most volunteers administered – or believed they were administering – what could easily have been lethal doses, even going as high as 450 volts. Milgram commented:

Men do become angry; they do act hatefully and explode in rage against others. But not here. Something far more dangerous is revealed: the capacity for man to abandon his humanity, indeed, the inevitability that he does so, as he merges his unique personality into larger institutional structures.[27]

Many, I am sure, will have difficulties with Milgram's use of that word 'inevitability'. We would do well, however, to reflect a little on what is likely to be involved in merging one's unique personality into the institutional structure. If this process amounts to losing one's autonomy, becoming something of an automaton, then perhaps 'inevitability' is not too strong a word. It is, of course, very useful that most humans have a strong tendency to obey. Anything less might lead to appalling chaos and injury in society. We have, moreover, already noted MacIntyre's claim that, most of the time, people grant willing obedience to the authority of political institutions because they see a coincidence between their own desires and those the satisfaction of which the authority is safeguarding. All of this, we might feel, is in the realm of common sense. Problems arise, however, when the tendency to obey, for whatever reason, is non-discriminatory or not sufficiently discriminatory, when people obey authority merely because it is authority. Unfortunately, it would seem that such a lack of discrimination and such automatic obedience are to be found, in varying degrees, in a very large percentage of humans. Evidently, we cannot reasonably expect to see significant improvement in this state of affairs unless there are notable changes in methods of upbringing and education. The traditional emphasis on obedience to authority to the detriment of personal responsibility is not helpful.

Lord Acton's claim that absolute power corrupts absolutely is most often quoted in discussions about authority in the ruling sense, although a somewhat modified version of the same adage

could perhaps also be applied to authority in the sense of expertise. It is important to note that, in both of these spheres, the
corruption is not always confined to the person in authority.
Much of the power wielded by such a person is lent, given by
or else stolen from those subject to authority. Now, lending a
certain amount of one's power conditionally to another person
or body of persons can, it would seem, be a wise procedure on
occasions. How else would present-day democracies function?
However, unquestioningly surrendering most of one's power
can mean, to a very large extent, surrendering one's autonomy.
Some might describe it as the selling of one's soul in exchange
for the sense of false security that comes from blind obedience
to the recipient of the power. It is surely true that protection
and dependence are both necessary in healthy human society,
but if we destroy or surrender autonomy, how can we have even
the beginnings of healthy human society? How can we ever have
healthy co-operation?

(b) Dissent

In recent years there has been a good deal of discussion concerning the rights and wrongs of dissent. For the sake of the common
good and for various other reasons, one should clearly not
indulge too easily and too lightly in dissent. That much would
seem to be beyond dispute, but the fact remains that, given the
appalling track record of the human race regarding both the
exercise of authority and the practice of destructive obedience,
a good deal more emphasis needs to be laid in such discussion
upon the virtue of sometimes disobeying. Difficulties arise when
special claims are made concerning a certain kind of authority
on the grounds that it comes directly from God. That was
certainly the case with the so-called 'divine right of kings'. The
rise of democracy has improved matters somewhat in recent
times, but the fact remains that, even in democracies, people
sometimes irresponsibly implement immoral decisions of their
governments merely because they have been told to do so.

Easy, but by no means the only, examples are found among the actions of those military personnel who implement appalling foreign-policy decisions of the democratically elected governments of powerful Western countries.

Within Protestantism there are now, one imagines, few, if any, fundamentalists of the kind who would quote biblical arguments in favour of slavery. This improved state of affairs has come about, no doubt, at least partly, through development in appreciation of what exactly biblical authority is. Having said that, however, we still need to bear in mind the facts that fundamentalism is alive and well and that many people still simplistically resort to the authority of Scripture regarding moral matters other than slavery. As an example we may take the way some appeal to the story of Sodom in Genesis as an authority in the debate about the rights and wrongs of homosexual behaviour, in spite of the unwholesome attitude to the rape of women that is found therein. Within Roman Catholicism, it would seem that there is need for more and deeper discussion about the authority of that Church's official teaching body, the *Magisterium*. Many, no doubt, will wish to point to the enormous achievements of that institution, but the fact remains that its track record with regard to such matters as slavery, the burning of heretics, religious liberty and the treatment of dissenters shows how dangerous could be a decision to obey too easily.

LEADERSHIP AND AUTHORITY

Some years ago Richard McCormick noted that there has been a tendency in the Church to identify authority and leadership. It may be that McCormick was speaking chiefly of the Roman Catholic Church, but the criticism could be applied over a much wider field, although perhaps not in a uniform way. When this identification is made in the thought patterns and usual operations of a group, says McCormick, there occurs, somewhat paradoxically, a factual separation between leadership and authority. This happens, he says, because, as reliance on mere authority increases, there is a decrease in the doing of those things which are required of true leadership. 'The result: as authority wanes, authority figures appeal all the more loudly to their authority and position.' He lists two results of careless identification of leadership with office:

> First, an independent value is attributed to mere office, with, of course, a dominant concern for the prerogatives of office and a corresponding insensitivity to the goals it serves. Secondly, we begin to experience the 'controlled' group or society. The symptoms of the controlled groups are well known: dominance of the negative in teaching; oppressive centralization at the administrative level; avoidance of risk in decision-making; derivativeness and enslavement to the traditional formula in theologizing; secretiveness in the use of power. The personality traits of the controlled group are equally well known: fear, anxiety, joyless security, rejection of risk, apathy.[28]

All of this adds weight, of course, to some of the conclusions of our previous section regarding obedience and dissent, but what are we to say about leadership? There are, says McCormick, many forms of leadership, but one element is common to all of them, and that is 'the release, stimulation, evocation, maximization of the potential of the individual. True leadership, in whatever form it is found, calls forth the best in those led. It *liberates* them into the fulness of their potential as individuals and as a group.' A person who has authority can conjoin leadership and authority by using the latter to liberate into its maximum potential the group that is in his or her care.[29]

DEALING WITH WHAT WE HAVE RECEIVED

As is the case with other matters discussed in this book, it can be quite misleading to talk of constant and unchanging Christian teaching regarding the ethics of authority. Changes inevitably came about, for instance, as people in general became more aware of the basic equality of all humans (males, females, aristocrats, peasants or whatever) and of the injustice of slavery. Other causes or catalysts of change have undoubtedly been the spread of democracy, the development of biblical scholarship, the dissemination of information about horrific war crimes and, of course, improvements in educational standards in many parts of the world. In spite of changes for the better which have occurred, however, we have no reason to be complacent about the content of teachings concerning authority that are disseminated in Christian circles or about the ways in which those teachings are passed on. What, perhaps, we should be most alarmed about are the facts that the problems of irresponsible obedience are not given anything like as much emphasis as the problems of dissent, and that, in some sections of Christianity, people are not sufficiently encouraged to develop their own consciences to make responsible decisions, but are instead urged to submit their wills blindly to bodies which they are told to regard as more or less infallible, in spite of the fact that those same bodies have made appalling errors in the past.

Earlier in this chapter I referred to the danger of allowing authority to dictate what should be taught about the nature and ethics of authority. When authority rules by fear, as it so often has done, even in the Church, it seems futile to talk about allowing authority to do anything. It simply does it, with or without our permission. However, when it is understood and exercised properly, it should be clear to everyone that the power which those in authority possess is freely given by those subject to authority, and that, when circumstances demand it, that power may, indeed should, be taken away. The corruption that does not come automatically from power comes very often all the same, and those in positions of either supposed or real ecclesiastical authority must take care not to blind themselves to the fact that this is just as true of the Church as it is of the state. If authority is to be redeemed, we need to take a new look at it and to see it, above all, in terms of a relationship between those exercising it and those being served by it. It is the demands of that relationship which must be met, not the demands of a real or imaginary tradition. Non-liberation, the stifling of human potential and the other ills of the controlled group listed by McCormick are alarming products of authority as it is so often wielded in this world of ours. At least equally alarming are the corrupting effects which can befall those in office. It is easy to understand how humans can come to rely upon such tools as dominance and fear in bringing order to society. It is especially sad, however, when those same tools are used, as they often have been,[30] in the Church of Christ, which preaches the gospel of liberation and love. It may well be unsettling to let the Spirit blow where she/he wills, but it is surely downright unchristian to attempt to replace that Spirit with something as weak and unstable as human authority. In saying that, I am not implying that there is no place for any kind of authority (well exercised and well respected) within the Church (as in other institutions and, of course, the state). Indeed, it is difficult to imagine how any human society could function without some sort of authority structure. No authority, however, should be treated as a substitute for the gospel or the Spirit.

NOTES

1. Alasdair MacIntyre, *A Short History of Ethics* (London: Routledge, 1991), p. 138.
2. R. P. Wolff, 'The conflict between authority and autonomy' in *Authority*, ed. Joseph Raz (Oxford: Basil Blackwell, 1990), p. 21.

3.   Helmut Thielicke, *Theological Ethics*, vol. 2: *Politics* (London: A. & C. Black, 1969), pp. 180–3.

4.   John N. Figgis, *The Divine Right of Kings* (Cambridge: Cambridge University Press, 1934), pp. 5–6.

5.   G. E. M. Anscombe, 'On the source of the authority of the state' in *Authority*, ed. Raz, pp. 144–5.

6.   Germain Grisez, *Christian Moral Principles*, vol. 1 of *The Way of the Lord Jesus* (Chicago: Franciscan Herald Press, 1983), p. 570.

7.   Ibid., pp. 849–56.

8.   Germain Grisez, *The Way of the Lord Jesus*, vol. 2: *Living a Christian Life* (Quincy, Illinois: Franciscan Press, 1993), p. 51.

9.   Grisez, *Christian Moral Principles*, p. 884.

10. Ibid., p. 220.

11. Robert P. George, 'Liberty under the moral law: B. Hoose's critique of the Grisez–Finnis theory of human good', *Heythrop Journal* 34 (1993), pp. 178–9. He is responding to Bernard Hoose, 'Proportionalists, deontologists and the human good', *Heythrop Journal* 33 (1992), pp. 175–91.

12. Grisez, *Christian Moral Principles*, p. 545. DV is an abbreviation of *Dei verbum*, which is the Dogmatic Constitution on Divine Revelation, a document of the Second Vatican Council.

13. Ibid., p. 900.

14. Gerald P. Fogarty, 'Dissent at Catholic University: The case of Henry Poels', *America* 155 (1986), pp. 180–4.

15. Nicholas P. Harvey, 'Women's ordination: A sideways look', *The Month* 252 (1991), pp. 232–3.

16. Ibid., p. 234.

17. Virginia Curran Hoffman, *The Codependent Church* (New York: Crossroad, 1991), p. 114.

18. Michael H. Crosby, *The Dysfunctional Church: Addiction and Codependency in the Family of Catholicism* (Notre Dame, Indiana: Ave Maria Press, 1991), p. 9.

19. Nicholas Peter Harvey, *The Morals of Jesus* (London: Darton, Longman & Todd, 1991), p. 65.

20. David B. Davis, *The Problem of Slavery in the Age of Revolution 1770–1823* (Ithaca and London: Cornell University Press, 1975), pp. 531–44.

21. Joseph Raz, 'Introduction' in *Authority*, ed. Raz, p. 3.

22. Robin Gill, *Christian Ethics in Secular Worlds* (Edinburgh: T. & T. Clark, 1991), p. 7.

23. 'Biblical Commission' in *The New Catholic Dictionary* (London: The Universal Knowledge Foundation, 1929), pp. 119–20.

24. James M. Gustafson, 'The place of Scripture in Christian ethics: A methodological study' in *Readings in Moral Theology* no. 4: *The Use of Scripture in Moral Theology*, ed. C. E. Curran and R. A. McCormick (New York: Paulist Press, 1984), p. 176.

25. William A. Henry III, 'The price of obedience', *Time* (3 February 1992), p. 21.

26. Ibid.

27. Stanley Milgram, *Obedience to Authority: An Experimental View* (New York: Harper & Row, 1974), pp. 188–9.

28. Richard A. McCormick, *Notes on Moral Theology 1965 Through 1980* (Washington DC: University Press of America, 1981), pp. 382–3.

29. Ibid., p. 383. He is commenting on and quoting from his own article 'Leadership and authority', *Proceedings of the Catholic Theological Society of America* 26 (1971).

30. In this regard we could cite as an example the tendency of popes in the not too distant past to use expressions like 'If anyone says . . . let him/her be accursed (*anathema sit*)'. We could also cite the tendency within the Roman Catholic Church, at least up to the time of the Second Vatican Council, to exercise control over people by declaring that they should perform a certain practice (e.g., attend Mass on a certain day) 'under pain of mortal sin'.

2

Concerning
Sex

Now we turn to a subject regarding which much ink has been spilt by innumerable people claiming to be either authorities or to have the backing of authority. Many who have spoken and written on the subject in recent times have given the impression that they have the backing of every major authority figure in the history of Christianity. Indeed, one could be forgiven for thinking that, from the point of view of conservative Christians (perhaps most especially, conservative Roman Catholics), there is little need for deviation from the wisdom of our ancestors where sexual ethics is concerned. The confidence with which statements are made about 'traditional' and 'unchanging' teachings in this sphere could easily lead one to think that such is the case. Interestingly, however, a little research reveals that most conservative scholars are not in agreement with some of the most basic tenets of the teachings of the great luminaries of past centuries concerning sexual ethics. Indeed, many of them, I feel sure, would be at pains to disassociate themselves from much that is in the writings of some of the greatest names in the history of Christianity. So too, I imagine, would many conservatives of a less scholarly bent if they but knew what those luminaries wrote on the subject. How, then, are we to explain that sense of certainty we detect in those who speak of a constant, unchanging tradition of Christian moral doctrine regarding human sexuality and sexual behaviour? This is an important question, and one to which we shall certainly return. Before that, however, we would do well to take a brief look at a number of the most significant items of real and supposed wisdom regarding human sex and sexuality expressed through the mouths and pens of some of our most influential forebears.

OUR SEXUAL INHERITANCE

The Bible

It has become fashionable in books on sexual ethics to highlight the generally positive approach to sex and sexuality that is to be found in the Bible. It is often said, for instance, that the very existence of the Song of Songs among the books of the Old Testament is a clear indication of the esteem in which erotic love was held. There is, of course, a long-established tradition of treating this particular work as an allegory of God's loving relationship with Israel, the Church and the individual Christian. Numerous biblical scholars, however, have pointed out in recent times that it is most unlikely that anything of the kind was the original intention of the book's author or authors. It is much more likely that it was intended to be no more than what it most evidently is – a poem, or collection of poems, in praise of erotic relationships. As such, they claim, it is eminently suitable material for what we have come to call Holy Scripture:

> Human sexual fulfillment, fervently sought and consummated in reciprocal love between woman and man: Yes, that is what the Song of Songs is about, in its literal sense and theologically relevant meaning. We may rejoice that Scripture includes such an explicit view among its various witnesses to divine providence.[1]

In addition to highlighting the Song of Songs, modern Christian writers on the subject of sexual ethics often mention the two creation narratives in Genesis. There, they say, it is clearly stated that God created sex, and indeed it was very good. The delight that lovers take in each other is seen as an important part of the divine plan. Moreover, the equality of the two sexes is fairly clearly stated, if not exactly underlined. Male and female are both included in the statement that humans are created in the image of God. In addition, some of these writers go on to mention the fact that the heterosexual union was held in such high esteem by the Israelites that it was used time and again as a metaphor for God's relationship with his people. All of this would appear to be true and very beautiful.

Passing on to the New Testament, we do not find an enormous amount of material on the subject of sex, but we do find approval of marriage in Jesus' attendance at a wedding feast and in his reiteration of a key text from Genesis: 'Have you not read that the Creator from the beginning made them male and female and that he said: This is why a man leaves his father and mother and becomes attached to his wife, and the two become one flesh?' (Matt 19:4–5). What is perhaps novel in the New Testament writings is St Paul's personal preference for celibacy, a matter to which we shall return later in this chapter.[2]

As we have already noted, there are good reasons for not turning to the Bible as the infallible and only guide on ethics. Nevertheless, modern writers on sexual ethics do well, it seems to me, in highlighting the differences between the generally positive attitude to sex and sexuality that is found in the Bible and the amazingly negative stance taken up by major Christian writers in later times. The question that springs to mind, then, is: if this negative stance had no basis in Scripture, on what was it founded? Where did it come from?

The Fathers of the Church

Many scholars, it would seem, are inclined to think that the correct answers to those questions are to be found in a few lines written by a group of British Quakers in 1963.

Only in the twentieth century have Christians dared in any
general way . . . to accept that, irrespective of any other purpose, coitus can be justified and dignified as the expression of
a deep relation between two persons. We do not blame Christianity and Christians of earlier centuries; we can seek the
origin of misconceived attitudes in the compromise between
pagan and Christian thought and in the social conditions of
the Dark Ages.[3]

No doubt many would classify as misleading any attempt
to cite Gnosticism as one of the most important instances of
such compromise. After all, the Gnostics were not orthodox
Christians. There are scholars, however, who suspect that those
who set out to purify the Church of Gnostic influences were not
as successful as some historical accounts may have led us to
believe. There were, of course, various types of Gnosticism,
but we can at least say that there was a common tendency in
the whole movement to regard the material world as evil and
the spiritual world as good – a dualism which, in various guises,
is also found in some other religions. Numerous Fathers of the
Church engaged in long and hard battles with the Gnostics.
Nevertheless, a number of scholars have suggested that some
of those same Fathers were themselves influenced more than
a little by the teachings of their opponents, so that they became
excessively wary of the sensual world in general and, more
particularly, took up a very negative and pessimistic stance
towards sex and sexuality. Others are perhaps a little more
cautious, and point merely to the fact that the differences
between the Fathers and the Gnostics on certain issues are not
as great as we might expect them to be. Derrick Sherwin Bailey
writes:

Although the church condemned the dualists for their
absolute rejection of matrimony, Christian thought upon sexual topics did not at all points conflict with that of Gnosticism

and Encratism. There is a similarity of language, and still more, of sentiment between patristic literature and the theosophies and apocryphal romances which makes it impossible to doubt that many of the Fathers were substantially at one with the extreme rigorists in their general *emotional* attitude to marriage and coitus.[4]

One of the more moderate of the patristic pessimists, it would seem, was St John Chrysostom.[5] Some time during the last quarter of the fourth century, he wrote a treatise on virginity in which he stated that, after the fall, humans were incapable of controlling their violent passions. Thus, in the Scriptures, we find God encouraging them to marry, to be fruitful and to multiply. In Chrysostom's opinion, commanding virginity and continence at that time would have resulted in disaster involving violent outbursts of passion. Virginity was therefore introduced only at a later stage for those who were strong. Marriage, it is true, was granted to humans, he writes, for the purpose of procreation, but there was also the greater reason of quenching our fiery passion. In other words, marriage originally had two purposes. Now that the whole world has been inhabited, however, only one of them remains, and that is the suppression of licentiousness and debauchery.[6]

Not many years later, Sulpitius Severus related a most revealing tale from the life of St Martin of Tours. One day when looking out over meadowland Martin noticed that oxen had eaten the grass in one part, that pigs had torn up bits and pieces with their snouts in another, and that a third area was untouched and sported flowers of various colours. The last mentioned portion of land, he announced, showed forth the glory of virginity, while the part which the pigs had dug up presented a picture of fornication. The portion in which the cattle had been exercising their jaws had not lost all the beauty of grass, but the grandeur of flowers had gone. This was a representation of marriage:

Thus, then, those who set marriage side by side with fornication grievously err; and those who think that marriage is to be placed on an equal footing with virginity are utterly wretched and foolish. But this distinction must be maintained by wise people, that marriage belongs to those things which may be excused, while virginity points to glory . . .[7]

A contemporary of both Sulpitius Severus and John Chrysostom was St Jerome, a man not renowned for moderation in language. He wrote in a letter that he valued marriage, but only because it caused virgins to be born. He picked the roses from the thorns.[8] Moreover, in his *Adversus Jovinianum*, while endeavouring to exalt virginity, Jerome spoke of marriage in such a derogatory way as to rob it of its dignity. Even St Augustine felt that Jerome had gone too far, and set about writing a treatise on the good of marriage. Any praise for the married state that he expresses in that work, however, is steeped in his generally pessimistic attitude towards sex. There is no fault attached to sexual intercourse, he informs us, if married people indulge in it for the purpose of generation. However, to take part in such activity beyond the needs of procreation, even in marriage, is a venial sin.[9]

Several scholars have noted that both Jerome and Augustine seem to have had their own quite serious problems in the sexual sphere. In view of the enormous influence that the writings of both had on later generations, we would do well, I think, to bear such things in mind. Jerome's biographer, J. N. D. Kelly, is of the opinion that self-knowledge and self-criticism were almost completely lacking to him. Jerome, he notes, used insulting language, misrepresenting Helvidius, for example, as an uncultivated boor, and telling another gentleman to hide his big nose and keep his mouth shut so that he might thereby appear to be handsome and an excellent speaker. In spite of this, however, in a letter to a friend, he asked (apparently, as far as he was concerned, in all innocence) if he had ever assailed anybody in bitter terms or spoken with excessive freedom.[10] Turning to the sexual sphere, Kelly describes him as strongly sexed, but also strongly repressed because of his convictions. He craved for female company, and, when he could have it without doing violence to those principles, he found deep satisfaction in it.[11] While it may be true that Jerome suffered from a serious lack of self-knowledge, his writings indicate that he was well aware of the fact that he was a highly sexed individual. At the same time, however, it does not seem that he was always aware of the ways in which his sexuality expressed itself, and he was probably totally unaware of the fact that savagely repressing sexual urges is not the healthiest way of dealing with them. He was also, I imagine, totally unaware of the fact that others would find it odd that he felt the need to praise virginity in quite such erotic language when writing on the subject to Eustochium, the third daughter of his close friend Paula.[12] It could be said that, in this instance, he was merely making use of the allegorical inter- pretation of the Song of Songs, as others had done before and many have done since. However, as Kelly points out, while it is true that both Ambrose and Augustine made use of the Song of Songs in their writings on virginity,

> the sexual overtones seem transposed in their exhortations. Jerome makes no attempt to play them down, and it is iron- ical to reflect that, in urging a young girl like Eustochium to crush the physical yearnings of her nature in the effort to surrender herself the more completely to Christ, he should feed her fantasy with such exciting images.[13]

Jerome's deep friendship with Eustochium's mother was obviously of enormous importance to him. If its depth was not evident to those around him during the last twenty years of Paula's lifetime, it must certainly have become so when she died. Kelly informs us that for several months he could not bring himself to do any literary work. In a letter to Theophilus, the Bishop of Alexandria, moreover, he declared that nothing could bring him consolation.[14] Regarding their relationship, Kelly writes that we would be naïve to deny that there was a sexual element in it, 'but it would be equally preposterous to infer that either party was aware of, still less gave overt expression to it'.[15] One is left wondering if Jerome might have modified his thinking regarding human sexuality had he only been aware of its positive role in his own life. Unfortunately, such self-awareness in that regard seems to have eluded him. Thus Bailey was able to write:

> His extravagant laudation of celibacy and his crude and violent outbursts against marriage, no less than the lascivious thoughts and visions which tormented him in his desert retreat, show that he never succeeded in coming to terms with his own sexuality. Even in the midst of his austerities he burned with desire as the scenes of his student dissipations arose before him, and a feverish imagination filled his cell with bevies of seductive girls. Both his confessions and his controversies proclaim a psychological unfitness to act as a guide in sexual matters, and his influence upon Christian thought in this respect can only be regretted.[16]

It may seem to many that Jerome's influence on the Christian Church regarding sexual matters has been slight in comparison to that of St Augustine. That, however, is a debatable point, not least because of Jerome's enormously influential translation of the Bible into Latin. On the other hand, one particularly negative and apparently influential piece of work for which Jerome has been blamed may not have been entirely the product of his negative stance regarding human sexuality. When he came to translate the book of Tobit he had access only to Aramaic texts. As he was unfamiliar with that language, he employed an interpreter who knew Hebrew and Aramaic. Jerome's translation, notes Kelly, depended heavily on the already existing Old Latin version. Moreover, 'on his own admission [he] treated the Aramaic pretty freely'. Whatever may be the reason, Jerome's rendering of Tobit contains material not found in any other text. We are told therein, for instance, that Tobias and his bride abstained from sexual intercourse for the first three nights of their marriage, although the original version states that they slept together on the first night. Kelly is of the opinion that, although Jerome would have heartily approved of advice to indulge in such abstention, 'it would be hazardous to assume that these expansions and re-writings represent contributions of his own'.[17] What is important here, however, is not the attribution of blame. It is the effect that this invention had on subsequent generations. Kelly notes that it had a considerable influence on the advice given to Roman Catholic newly-weds until quite recent times.[18] Uta Ranke-Heinemann, moreover, sees it introducing a note of sexual pessimism into the book of Tobit, although 'sexual pessimism had no place in the Judaism of the Old Testament'.[19] Its influence probably became less widespread after the Reformation as Protestants demoted the book of Tobit to the ranks of the non-canonical texts.

Another sexual pessimist and scholar who does not seem to have been able to come to terms with his own sexuality was Tertullian. In spite of his lack of orthodoxy, he too seems to have had considerable influence on subsequent generations. His pessimism is especially evident in a short passage in his treatise *De exhortatione castitatis*. Marriage and fornication, he asserts, are different only in the degree of their illegitimacy. That is because sexual relations are involved in both, and, according to Tertullian, our Lord says that the very desire to indulge in that kind of activity is the same thing as fornication. In answer to the objection that such doctrine is destructive of all marriage, he says that there is good reason for being so destructive because, in the shameful act which constitutes its essence, marriage is the same as fornication.[20]

One of the most influential of the Fathers was, of course, the great Augustine. In his case too, it seems, we have a man who did not deal well with his own sexuality. In the days of his youth he was quite active sexually, sometimes, apparently, with other men's wives. Eventually, he entered into a relationship with a woman whose name we do not know. She bore him a son, and the relationship lasted some thirteen years. She was, however, socially inferior, a fact which apparently ruled out marriage. When, somewhat under the influence of his mother, he came to see the expediency of getting married, he looked elsewhere and sent the poor woman back to Africa, while retaining custody of their son. As the girl chosen to be his bride was not yet old enough for marriage, the sex-hungry Augustine found himself another mistress. In his experience, writes Virginia Curran Hoffman, 'sex was not an expression of committed love and deepening relationship; sex was a need, a drive, a hunger. He used women to satisfy that hunger.'[21] The stories that have come down to us concerning his sexual escapades before his conversion would certainly seem to indicate the accuracy of such a statement. What, however, is to be said about his general attitude towards sex after his conversion?

In Hoffman's opinion – with which, I imagine, many scholars would concur – Augustine was a sex addict. Now, in addiction circles, she notes, it is normal to distinguish between abstinence (merely doing without the substance or process involved) and true sobriety or recovery. It is possible to abstain without really dealing with the source of the problem. A person who does that, and who is sometimes referred to in the context of alcohol addiction as a 'dry drunk', 'displays the same negativity and craziness as before, but without the chemical'. In order to attain true sobriety, she continues, one must take part in a recovery programme 'that will help one replace old destructive attitudes and behaviors with another, healthier set of beliefs'. Applying this line of thinking to Augustine, Hoffman concludes that he 'was an abstinent, but *not recovering*, sex addict. His theology betrays the obsession of an addict.' In fact, she goes on to say, his obsession with sex was just as strong after his conversion as before it. 'Taken all together, Augustine's ideas about sex sound like the ravings of a "dry drunk".'[22]

This may seem surprising in view of the fact, already noted above, that Augustine wrote a treatise in praise of marriage to counterbalance Jerome's excesses in the latter's *Adversus Jovinianum*. It is true that Augustine does have some positive things to say about marriage in that document, but, at the same time, he evidently regrets that sex is in any way associated with it, unless it is used exclusively for producing babies. Thus, as already noted, we find him writing that, even within marriage, to indulge in sexual intercourse beyond the need for generation is a venial sin. Elsewhere he says that husband and wife cannot participate in the honourable and permitted embrace that is necessary for generation unless they are fired by the ardour of concupiscence. This ardour is not the servant of the will. It is not excited by a movement of the will, but by a seductive stimulus, and, on that account, it produces shame. This carnal concupiscence, he says, is, as it were, the daughter of sin. When, moreover, it gives assent to shameful deeds, it becomes the mother of many sins. As a result of this concupiscence, whoever is born naturally is bound by original sin unless that person is born again into him whom the Virgin conceived without concupiscence.[23] In explaining Augustine's thought, John Bugge writes: 'To have been "conceived in sin" meant that the act was accomplished "in" – by means of – *libido*.' The sin, he goes on to say, lay not in copulation itself, but in the lust that accompanied it. This fine distinction makes it possible to retain the force of the Gnostics' identification of sin with sexuality, and, at the same time, to deal with the Gnostics' claim that evil is vested in matter:

> With Augustine the flesh is not absolutely evil, but only in proportion to the degree to which the will has allowed it to become dominant. The distinction between the two

positions, of course, is fundamental, but the effect of each upon Christian practice over the course of centuries was destined – perhaps ironically – to be much the same.[24]

A passage in *De Genesi ad litteram* reveals a good deal about Augustine's attitude towards women and the possibility of deep relationships between the sexes. In a discussion about the creation of Eve, he asks in what way the woman was to be a helper to the man if she was not made to help in the begetting of children:

> She was not to till the earth with him, for there was not yet any toil to make help necessary. If there were any such need, a male helper would be better, and the same could be said of the comfort of another's presence if Adam were perhaps weary of solitude. How much more agreeably could two male friends, rather than a man and a woman, enjoy companionship and conversation in a life shared together . . . Surely no one will say that God was able to make from the rib of the man only a woman and not also a man if He had wished to do so. Consequently, I do not see in what sense the woman was made as a helper for the man if not for the sake of bearing children.[25]

It might be objected at this point that I have not been entirely fair to the patristic authors whose writings I have discussed. After all, there were, undoubtedly, other factors at work of which I have made no mention. One such factor, mentioned by Eric Fuchs, is the influence of Stoicism on Christian ethical discourse. Christians of ancient times, he notes, found an elaborate and lofty ethical system among the Stoics, and shared with them the same criticism of sexual customs of their time. Theologians borrowed the Stoic notion of natural law, which made it possible for them to have an objective moral standard. Christianity, however, also inherited the Stoics' distrust of imagination and passion. The Stoics, moreover, continues Fuchs, were wary of tender affection:

> If tender affection can be considered weakness, how much more should one indeed guard against sexual desire! This is why one must be careful about love. 'Any love for another's wife is scandalous; likewise too much love for one's spouse is adultery. The wise man should love his wife with his head (with discernment, *iudicis*), not with his heart (not with affection, *non affectu*). He should control his passions and not let himself be dragged along into intercourse. Nothing is more impure (*foedius*) than to love one's wife like a mistress. Surely those who claim to unite themselves to their wives to beget children for the good of the State or for the human race should at least imitate the animals and once their wives are pregnant not destroy the offspring. Let them approach their wives as husbands and not as lovers.' This surprising passage from Seneca has come down to us only through Jerome's respectful quoting of it. He precedes this quote with one from Sextus the Pythagorian whose original text he corrects: 'An adulterer is also he who is shamelessly immodest with his own wife.' This quote becomes a formula that is closer to Seneca: 'An adulterer is one who too passionately loves his wife.' This sentence will often be quoted, with complete approval, by Christian moralists up until the time of Gratian and Peter Lombard. We find an almost identical version of the saying in Augustine: 'For he who is intemperate in marriage, what is he but the adulterer of his own wife?'[26]

John Noonan notes that the use of Stoic values in the appeal to nature served as a way of reacting to the general social environment of the time in which it seemed to Christian writers that sexual pleasure was often pursued in an uncontrolled way. They lived in a world in which slave concubinage flourished, divorce was easy and homosexuality was frequently practised.

Thus it seemed to them that they found the opposite of that holy control which is recommended by the Gospels and St Paul. 'The test of procreative purpose seemed to many Christians, as it had to the pagan Stoics and to reflective Jews like Philo, the measure by which sexual promiscuity might be rationally criticized.' Thus, he continues, the reaction to sexual licence helped to reinforce the commitment to Stoic–Jewish rules which had been made to appear essential by the Gnostic polemic.[27]

Some may feel that, in order to avoid accusations of being ahistorical or at least not historical enough, I should continue in this vein for many more pages. I should, however, point out that my chief aim in this section is not a criticism of the teachings of the Fathers in their own time. What matters, for the purposes of this chapter, is the effects of those teachings which have been passed on to us, and, of course, what is to be said about present-day claims regarding continuing, unchanging and unchangeable teachings regarding sex and sexuality in the light of what we have seen in the teachings of the Fathers.

Later Developments

It is sometimes said that the writings of Thomas Aquinas on the subject of human sexuality have a more positive ring to them than those of Jerome or Augustine. There is some truth in this, but anybody looking for an enormous improvement is likely to be disappointed. In one place, for instance, Thomas lifts the spirit of the reader just a little by referring to the need for equality in the friendship that husbands and wives should have.[28] In another place, however, we find him upholding the thesis that the marital embrace is defiling. He says there that sexual pleasure puts more pressure on our reasoning faculties than does the pleasure which comes from eating. Consequently, a much greater effort is needed to restrain and correct the former. The more one consents to it, the greater becomes the power of concupiscence, and the power of the mind is brought down. Without further comment, he then reminds us that

Augustine knew of nothing that brings down the manly spirit so much as the caresses without which a woman cannot be cherished.[29] Elsewhere he says that the evil which is associated with and inseparable from carnal intercourse is not sin but punishment consisting in the non-submission of concupiscence to reason. The turpitude that is always present in the act of marriage and which makes us feel ashamed results from punishment, not sin. Humans are naturally ashamed of any defect.[30]

Bailey feels that it is most unlikely that ordinary men and women of medieval times appreciated or were even aware of the subtle arguments used by Scholastic theologians to distinguish moral evil from other forms of evil. They may well have been instructed that the regenerative and remedial uses of sex were not blameworthy, but the general impression left on simple and unlearned people must have been

> that the physical relationship of the sexes was regarded by religion as unworthy, if not as shameless and obscene. The effect of such teaching must necessarily have been grave; it caused a distortion of principles and values which has left an indelible mark upon Christian sexual thought, and we can only guess at the psychological disturbances and conflicts which it produced in the lives of individuals.[31]

A certain amount of change came with the Protestant Reformation. In varying degrees the Reformers praised marriage and played down or, in some cases, even denied the superiority of celibacy. An important point to note, however, is the fact that, for a long time, leaders within the Reformed denominations continued to teach that the purpose of sexual intercourse was procreation. Moreover, in spite of the new Protestant praise for marriage and a growing tendency within Catholicism to depart from the more pessimistic notions of Augustine (the impetus for such movement perhaps coming largely from the fact that Luther was strongly influenced by Augustine), a general air of prudishness and sexual alarm seems to have swept through both camps during the latter half of the sixteenth century, partly at least, where Catholics were concerned, as a reaction to the licence of Renaissance Italy, especially under the Borgias. Paul IV, for instance, ordered that all the nudes in Michelangelo's Sistine Chapel paintings should be covered with draperies. Early in the seventeenth century, moreover, the General of the Jesuits announced to all members of his Society that they were not to teach that there could be 'parvity of matter' where venereal misdemeanours were concerned.[32] In other words, all such transgressions had the potential to be mortal sins. Nothing in the sphere of sex was trivial. As for Protestantism, Bailey reports that the liberating influence of the Reformation was to some extent neutralized by a certain 'puritanism' with regard to sexual matters. Prudishness showed itself in a tendency among Protestants to regard sexual sins with severity, a severity which was intensified, he continues, by a lively awareness of the God who had ordained marriage as the remedy for human incontinence.[33] As in the case of Catholicism, there was apparently a reaction to licence here. There were, however, to be various swings within the different branches of the Reform movement until recent times:

> The excesses of the Anabaptists in Germany encouraged moral strictness in Lutheranism and even more in Pietism. In Britain and America attitudes of English Puritan and Scots Kirk harshness, followed by Restoration licence, led on to Victorian prudery and modern revolt. There were many cross- and counter-currents, theological as well as moral. The dominance of both Evangelical piety and Broad Church laxity in the eighteenth century, was met by High Church revival in the nineteenth century praising clerical celibacy and exalting virginity. Then new forces gathered together to produce demands for revised sexual teachings today.[34]

Such swings and counter-swings do not, of course, always indicate development, and that would certainly seem to have been
the case here. In the post-Reformation period, some individuals
and groups did take steps forward, but one would need to read
the history of sexual ethics with glasses of the rosiest tint to see
signs of any major widespread improvement in the situation
before the twentieth century, and, even then, progress was
slow. Within Catholicism, moreover, from the seventeenth century onwards, the officially condemned but influential Jansenist
movement reinforced pessimistic notions about sex, and, even
today, some continuing effects of that movement are easy to
identify.

To make matters worse, a batch of widely read scientific and
pseudo-scientific literature published in the eighteenth and
nineteenth centuries spoke of sex in very negative terms. In
1760 the Swiss physician Tissot published a book which had
enormous influence. In it he stated that masturbation caused
various disorders, including paralysis, epilepsy, deterioration of
eyesight and insanity. Numerous other doctors of medicine
joined in to provide an alarming chorus in various parts of the
Western world.[35] 'In 1867, one of the greatest British physi-
cians of his time, Henry Maudsley, said that masturbation was
characterized by extreme perversion and derangement of
thought. He also maintained that masturbation was the cause
of low intelligence, hallucinations, and suicidal and homicidal
tendencies.'[36] Even well into the twentieth century, it was not
impossible to find efforts being made to establish a connection
between masturbation and insanity.[37] How much the research
of scientists was compromised by inherited prejudices concerning sex is impossible to say. What matters is that numerous
members of the scientific community helped to reinforce the
commonly held view that sex was in some way evil.

Before moving on to a consideration of twentieth-century
developments, it might be useful to note that some scholars
would wish to highlight the importance of factors other than

those so far mentioned which played an important part in influencing the teachings of our forebears. James Nelson, for instance, writes:

> Augustine was a primary theological shaper of the procreative norm as central to sexuality's meaning. But we need to understand his thought in the historical-social context of threat to the family. Maternal and infant mortality was exceedingly high, the economic and political structures were based on kinship, and the family seemed to be the only dependable social unit in a time of civil wars and barbarian invasions. Likewise, clerical celibacy was in part shaped by the economic interests of the church: single male clergy would not produce offspring who in turn would fight over church property. So also the prohibitions against homosexuality were in part grounded in the interests of a male church hierarchy in preserving its rational ordering unaffected by the passions of personal-sexual ties. And the antipleasure climate of Victorian sexuality in part was shaped by the need of the Industrial Revolution for a public morality of hard work, dedication, and delayed gratification.[38]

Discussion of such factors may help us to understand a little better how people of former times came to teach as they did on sexual matters. However, it does not show their teaching to be less wrong than would be the case without such background information. Nor does it in any way reduce the urgency of our need to liberate ourselves from the negative influences of faulty doctrines from the past.

CHANGES IN TEACHING

In the early years of the twentieth century, it seems, there was within Anglicanism a good deal of opposition to the growing birth-control movement. In 1908 the Lambeth Conference

warned against the use of artificial means of avoiding conception.[39] The 1920 Conference declined to lay down rules for
every abnormal case, but regarded with grave concern the
spread of theories and practices which were hostile to the family.
An emphatic warning was issued against the use of unnatural
means of avoiding conception, and Anglicans were reminded
that the primary purpose of marriage is the continuance of the
race.[40] However, at the next Conference, in 1930, a majority
(193 to 67) voted in favour of a resolution agreeing that, where
there is a clearly felt need to avoid or limit parenthood, and
where there are morally sound reasons for avoiding complete
abstinence, other methods may be used in the light of Christian
principles. Once again, however, it was stated that the primary
purpose of marital union is procreation.[41] A major development came at the 1958 Conference when the primacy of procreation was rejected, the personal value of sexual intercourse was
emphasized and the notion that it was evil was condemned.[42]

> The 'theology of St Augustine', too, was no longer,
> apparently, acceptable – though in stating this, the Report
> observed that 'the Church holds as strongly as ever that con-
> tinence, chastity, and self-control are a positive and creative
> element in Christian living'. It was quite a volte-face. All the
> qualifications which had accompanied the 1930 Lambeth
> ruling that contraception could be permitted only in cases of
> exceptional social or medical need were abandoned. Contra-
> ception was now to be freely allowed because of the human
> values implicit in sexual union. This was a revolution in the
> Church's attitude to sexual morality.[43]

Numerous Protestant churches came to accept that the use
of artificial contraception within marriage was conformable to
Christian ideals, but there was resistance to such developments
within the Greek Orthodox Church. As for Roman Catholicism,
Vincent Genovesi notes that, by the middle of the nineteenth

century, it is possible to identify three stages in Church teaching regarding the proper motivation of married couples for engaging in sexual intercourse. The first was that the couple should have a procreative intention. In the second stage 'it was proposed that other motives for intercourse are morally acceptable so long as couples do not positively exclude the intention of procreation'. With the third stage came acceptance of the fact that couples could legitimately engage in sexual intercourse while intending and desiring to avoid procreation, provided they did not directly and deliberately interfere with the procreative potential of the act.[44] The third stage may have been identifiable by the middle of the nineteenth century, but, as Genovesi acknowledges, it was not officially publicized until the middle of the twentieth. In an address to the Italian Catholic Society of Midwives in 1951, Pius XII gave official approval to the use of the 'safe period'. If they had a good enough reason for doing so, Catholic couples could restrict their sexual activity to the times in the woman's cycle when she was infertile.

In spite of the development of the above-mentioned third stage, it was generally taught within the Roman Catholic Church, until the Second Vatican Council, that procreation was the primary end of the conjugal act. Such terminology was abandoned at the Council and has not been resurrected since. Without referring to one as primary and the other as secondary, recent documents of the Catholic *Magisterium* have insisted that there are two ends of sexual intercourse within marriage: the unitive and the procreative. It is stated in these same documents, however, that these two ends must never be separated. According to the *Magisterium*'s interpretation of natural law as God's law written in nature, any use of artificial contraceptives with the intention of avoiding conception does just that. The same kind of thinking is applied to artificial insemination using the husband's sperm.

THE PRESENT SITUATION

Earlier in this chapter we left unanswered the question how we are to explain the sense of certainty in those who speak of a constant, unchanging tradition of Christian moral teaching regarding human sexuality. After our glance at history, it seems to me that we have no alternative than to say that such 'certainty' is not well founded. Tradition, however, plays a big part in human affairs, and, as far as Christianity is concerned, that is especially true of the Roman Catholic Church. A belief that one's Church is and always has been true to the gospel can, understandably, cause one to overlook even the most obvious differences between one's own convictions and those of one's predecessors. If we may turn from the subject of sexuality for a moment, that perhaps explains a mistake made by Leo XIII. In 1890, in a letter addressed to the bishops of the whole world, he wrote that many of his predecessors – twelve of whom he named – had made every effort to ensure that the institution of slavery would be abolished. While expressing the greatest respect for Leo, John Maxwell wrote that the Pope's claim was historically inaccurate. All twelve of the popes named by him had condemned only what they held to be *unjust* methods of enslavement or *unjust* titles of slave-ownership. Moreover, five of those popes were the authors of documents which authorized enslavement either as an institution or as a consequence of war or as a penalty for ecclesiastical crimes.[45] Now, it would seem that a somewhat similar overlooking of the facts has been happening in the sphere of sexual ethics. Who, Catholic or Protestant, could seriously claim to represent a tradition of teaching on such matters which has not changed since the time of the Fathers? I am inclined to think that if we were to teach as valid some of the excesses of certain Fathers of the Church, we would most certainly have something to be ashamed of, and it would not be our sexuality. One wonders, moreover, how many of the Fathers, and, indeed, how many of the great Christian luminaries from much later eras, would have been entirely happy with the following statement resulting from the Second Vatican Council:

> Married love is uniquely expressed and perfected by the exercise of the acts proper to marriage. Hence the acts in marriage by which the intimate and chaste union of the spouses takes place are noble and honourable; the truly human performance of these acts fosters the self-giving they signify and enriches the spouses in joy and gratitude.[46]

The belief that there is a healthy continuity with the teachings of the ancients can, of course, lead to problems. Any changes of direction have to be presented as developments rather than as breaks with the past. In the case of sexual ethics, however, such a procedure leaves us with a very important question. If there has been no break with those teachings of St Jerome and others that we discussed above, are we to conclude that present-day teachings have the same foundation as those earlier ones? In other words, are we to conclude that the teachings of those Christian bodies which have not made a break with clearly erroneous teachings of another age are based on a belief that sex and sexuality are basically evil? One can imagine howls of protest greeting such a suggestion, but it is difficult, to say the least, to see how one can claim to be faithful to an unchanging tradition unless one does have such a basis for one's sexual ethics. More specifically, if, in some quarters, there is still insistence that all acts of sexual intercourse should be open to procreation, what grounds do we have for holding that what is being taught is more than just a modified version of an earlier teaching that only the intention to have children could make such acts justifiable? Any attempt to prove that something other than a modified version of the earlier teaching is involved would obviously imply a break with past teaching, but, if that were the case, claims about a constant and unbroken tradition would be empty. This is important if it means that present teachings on such matters as homosexual relations, contraception and celibacy have a very shaky foundation.[47] We could also add teachings on marriage and heterosexual extra-marital relations to the list, because marriage, according to the 'wisdom' of some of our most illustrious ancestors, was a licence to indulge in what would otherwise be appalling activity. Interestingly, it might be thought that divorce should not be mentioned here because traditional teaching (and present-day teaching of the Roman Catholic *Magisterium* regarding this matter) is based on a fundamentalist reading of certain passages from the New Testament. Some, however, may be inclined to think that the temptation to indulge in such fundamentalist reading may have been strengthened in the early centuries of the Church's history by the tendency of numerous Fathers of the Church to discourage people from entering into second marriages even after the death of their spouses.

Whatever our conclusions may be regarding such matters, the fact remains that most of us were born into a world in which Christian teachings about sex were steeped in pessimism, a world, some would say, in which so-called Christian teachings about human sex and sexuality were not really all that Christian. Furthermore, psychology has taught us a good deal about the damage that can be done by denying that we are sexual beings, by suppressing our sexual urges instead of facing up to them, by refusing to embrace and rejoice in our sexuality. Again we are left with one of those unanswerable questions. Which has caused the most damage: sexual licence or sexual suppression and the labelling of sex as dirty?

THE NEED TO THINK AGAIN

It would be worth doing anything to rescue sex from what it is to most of my generation, a murky and furtive secret. I am afraid it cannot be completely done. The Victorian

curse and taboos are too hard to overcome. And of course
much that we want to sweep away goes back to earlier days;
much, indeed, to the days of early Christianity . . . The flesh
belonged to this world. It was evil. Sex and sin were synony-
mous. So Christianity grew up with an attitude to sex from
which many are not, even now, emancipated. But I believe
emancipation could be achieved for the rising generation. If
only sex could be presented to them so that their reaction to
it was as clean and joyous and radiant as their reaction to the
splendour of a summer dawn! . . . Religion and psychology,
faith and science need to be yoked together and intelligently
applied in order that sex, to many people still an unclean
thing, may become what surely the God who implanted it
meant it to be.[48]

The above passage comes from a book which was first published
in 1931. Since then there has been a so-called sexual revolution
in various parts of the world, but it would seem that, even now,
the reaction of a large percentage of the human race to sex
is not yet anything like as clean, joyous and radiant as their
reaction to the splendour of a summer dawn.

In view of the fact that a generally positive attitude towards
human sexuality is to be found in the Bible, it is understandable
that some people might suggest that the solution to our problem
lies in the pages of Holy Scripture. However, as we saw earlier,
if that means treating the Bible as an infallible manual of moral
theology, such a procedure can lead us into quite unethical
'solutions'. In the debate about the ethics of homosexual relations, for example, people on both sides have made use of the
story of Sodom and Gomorrah. Some people see it as a clear
condemnation of genital activity between members of the same
sex (at least as far as males are concerned). Others point to the
fact that the story is more complicated than that because the
men hammering at Lot's door and demanding to have sex with
his visitors are clearly intending rape. Also underlined by some

is the obvious lack of hospitality, which would have been viewed as a serious matter. What often seems to be ignored by many people on both sides of the debate, however, is the fact that Lot cries out to the would-be rapists: 'Please, brothers, do not be wicked. Look, I have two daughters who are virgins. I am ready to send them out to you, for you to treat as you please, but do nothing to these men since they are now under the protection of my roof' (Gen 19: 8). The reader is apparently to infer that sending out the girls in these circumstances would be the lesser of two evils. I imagine that few people today who call themselves Christians would be happy with that. I also imagine that few would be entirely happy with what Deuteronomy has to say about the case of a man who seizes a young virgin who is not betrothed and sleeps with her. If he is caught in the act, the rapist must give fifty silver shekels to the girl's father. More-over, 'since he has exploited her, she must be his wife and, as long as he lives, he may not divorce her' (Deut 22:28–29). This is to be contrasted with the case of a man who has sex with a girl who is betrothed. If this happens in the town, both of them are to be stoned to death: the man for exploiting another man's wife, and the girl for not having called for help. If, on the other hand, the man rapes the girl in the open country, where nobody can hear her cries for help, only he should die (Deut 22:23–27). William Graham Cole concludes from this:

> The rape itself was not so serious. It was the violation of another man's rights which was of concern. The rape of a betrothed woman was tantamount to adultery, and therefore merited death. But the rape of an unbetrothed girl could be expiated by marriage, though the husband had forfeited his right to divorce. Once more, the rights of the male asserted themselves.[49]

Again we see that, whatever may be said about biblical insights providing a basic orientation, we would be unwise to resort to

Scripture too easily as the ultimate authority on particular issues in the sphere of ethics.

In building on the wisdom of our forebears, I think we usually assume that we are building on what they learned, at least in part, from experience. If, however, we were merely trying to build on the 'traditional' teachings we have discussed so far in this chapter, we would surely not be building on experience at all. Instead, our foundations would be strange theories which most, perhaps all, of us would reject. On the other hand, learning from experience is not always as easy as one might think. For instance, we could include under the heading of experience the contributions of the various sciences, but, unfortunately, as we have already seen, until quite recent times, a good deal of what came from the scientific community regarding human sex and sexuality was not well developed, parts of it not presented in a balanced way, and much of it certainly not scientific. Even if we were to limit ourselves to the purely procreational sphere, it seems that little worthwhile progress was made in biological discovery until recent times. As for the relational aspects of human sexuality, it appears that very little serious study was done – at least in the Western world – until the time of Sigmund Freud.[50] Another problem about experience is that it does not take place in a vacuum. The negative teachings we have discussed doubtless had some effect on a good deal of human sexual experience over many centuries. To illustrate the importance of that, we might leave aside the subject of sex and sexuality for a moment and take up the example of a man who is afraid of darkness, the fear having been instilled during childhood by adults who often spoke to him about goblins, imps and other nasty creatures that supposedly stalk our world after sundown. Suppose that some scientists decide to find out whether there is anything in darkness itself that could cause humans to be afraid. On its own, that man's experience of darkness would be of limited value. Apparently, he has experienced it as something to be afraid of only because other people caused him to fear it. Had they not done so, would he have had reason to be afraid, or, more simply, would he have been afraid? Research will obviously have to go beyond his experience and the experience of people with similar histories to his. Something similar can be said regarding a person's experience of sex when that person has been told since childhood that sex is evil. In other words, we need to tread very carefully, admitting, it seems to me, that, at this moment in time, we know very little about our subject.

Of course, it could be objected that the wisdom of the ancients has not yet had a thoroughly fair hearing in this chapter. After all, in spite of what present-day scholars may have to say about Gnostic, Stoic and other influences upon early Christian thought, it is just possible that experience too indicated that celibacy was to be preferred to marriage because sex was *experienced* as essentially evil. It might be said in support of such a theory that we need only look around us and read a few newspapers to see a great deal of damage to people that is caused sexually. On the other hand, it could also be said that, adopting the same course of action, we would become aware of an immense amount of damage caused to people largely as a result of the abuse of intelligence – fraud and various kinds of plots being among the more spectacular examples. One imagines that we would not be expected to conclude from this that intelligence is evil. What is important in both cases is surely the abuse of the human faculty concerned. Of course, it could be claimed that, because of our brokenness, our sexual faculties are corrupted, but again, the same would have to be said about our intellectual powers. In other words, experience does not indicate that sex is any more evil than intelligence, and, of course, intelligence, or the human capacity to reason, is one of the 'sacred cows' of Christian tradition. Indeed, one of the major problems with sex, according to some of our forebears, is its supposed tendency to fetter our reasoning powers.[51]

With the case against sex not proven, let us now turn to the

question of celibacy. St Paul tells us that he has no instruction
from the Lord regarding this matter, but that he is of the opinion that celibacy is preferable to marriage. Unmarried people,
he says, concentrate their minds on God's business and how
to please the Lord, whereas married people are concerned
with how to please their spouses and with affairs of the world
(1 Cor 7:25–35). Some might wish to suggest at this point that,
had Paul known what we know about the petty concerns and
jealousies that have abounded in so many convents, monas-
teries, friaries and presbyteries, he might not have spoken with
such confidence on the matter.

In practice, not all celibates are free of ties. Some, for example, have to look after the children of relatives who have died.
For celibates who do not have such commitments, however,
there are obvious advantages, such as greater freedom of movement, which, to use traditional language, can be exploited for
the Kingdom. As for those who are married, on the other hand,
the self-giving involved in their way of life could equally be said
to be of enormous benefit to the Kingdom. Thus we have
two ways of life which can be taken up for the Kingdom. This
is all very clear and easy to understand. Some statements
made about celibacy and the Kingdom, however, particularly
in Roman Catholic circles, might be thought by some to have
verged on the esoteric, even in recent times. In an encyclical
letter on the Catholic priesthood published in 1935, for example, Pius XI says, regarding celibacy, that, since God is Spirit,
it is fitting that somebody who is dedicated and consecrated to
God's service should in some way 'divest himself of his body'.
As he then goes on to speak about ancient Roman and Hebrew
practices,[52] there are reasonable grounds for thinking that he is
merely discussing ritual purity. However, as such references to
'uncleanness' are out of place in a Christian document, one can
only conclude that the old unhealthy notion that sex is essentially evil was having its effect on the Pope.

The practice of celibacy has been encouraged, not only in

Christianity, but also among Buddhists and Jains. Indeed, Buddhism was originally principally for monks. That fact might be thought to be not all that significant. After all, various forms of asceticism are found in many religions. That some of them should include celibacy as part of their asceticism is not surprising. On the other hand, it could be that, at some stage, contemplative souls in all three movements (Christianity, Jainism and Buddhism) saw sex as an obstacle to contemplation. If they also regarded contemplatives as the most perfect of humans, it would be easy to understand why they might have encouraged people to be celibate. Whether sex is or is not an obstacle to certain kinds of meditation and contemplation – at least for some people – is a matter for debate. It is worth noting, however, that there are married contemplatives. It is also worth noting that, in much discourse, the word contemplation is not confined to the divine gift referred to by some of the great Christian mystics, but is used in reference to certain states of consciousness which can be brought about at will by people who have undergone the requisite training. It is fairly obvious that having the ability to enter into such states of consciousness does not necessarily indicate that one is more fully human, more of a saint, if you like, than most other people. Moreover, having said all this, we should not ignore the possibility that sexual intercourse is a mystical experience for some people.

It does not seem to be at all clear, then, that either way of life is superior to the other. It seems even less clear that sex is essentially evil. Indeed many people have, no doubt, experienced it as entirely good, thoroughly positive. Moreover, most Christian bodies today would agree with the statement that sex is not essentially evil. They – at least, some, perhaps most, of them – would seem to have a problem, however, in that they have broken away from the foundation upon which 'traditional' teaching was based, but still claim some sort of continuity with that teaching. That is clear for all to see, in various denominations, when the subjects of homosexual relations and extra-marital heterosexual activity are debated. It is also clear, most especially in Roman Catholicism, when artificial contraception, masturbation and 'unnatural' sexual activity in general are debated.

We have already had reason to refer to the roles of science and human experience in ethics and to the fact that, where sexual ethics is concerned, there are bound to be difficulties in gathering data from these sources. We can, however, make a start. Some of the findings of psychology, for instance, have emphasized for us the importance of intimacy. Clearly, not all of our intimate relationships could or should be described as erotic, but our sexuality does incline us towards forming attachments. Here again it might be thought that we are running into difficulties with traditional Christian teaching, which speaks of detachment, especially in the context of the so-called evangelical counsels of chastity, poverty and obedience. The problem is largely one about the meanings of words. There can be an enormous difference between taking and possessing on the one hand and freely giving and receiving on the other. In the one case, there may be no growth at all, just a turning in on oneself and a compulsion to acquire more and more things and persons in order to satisfy one's cravings. In the other case, there is mutual discovery and the finding of the Spirit of Love that lives in the two personalities. Discovery of the other person, of course, also involves discovery of self and that same Spirit of Love within oneself.

In the sexual sphere, more, perhaps, than in any other branch of Christian ethics, there has been a widespread tendency to hold that certain actions are wrong only because God forbids them. This is, of course, quite different from saying that God forbids certain actions because they are wrong. There would seem to be more than a hint of that kind of thing in much that is said about natural law and so-called 'unnatural' sexual activity. God's law, we are told, is written in nature. Occasionally one hears it admitted by supporters of this point of view that the natural law arguments supplied so far regarding the claimed wrongness of artificial contraception and various other activities have failed to convince. Other arguments, it is said, must be found. Normally, conclusions are based on arguments, but, in this case, it would seem, the conclusion has been reached in some other way, and arguments must be found which will fit that conclusion. In its traditional forms, says Gareth Moore, the appeal to nature always comes after the determination of what may or may not be done sexually. He also points out that our perception of what is natural is shaped in large part by pre-existing social norms.[53]

If, of course, one abandons the notion that certain forms of sexual activity are wrong only because God forbids them and accepts rather that God forbids certain actions because they are wrong, one must have criteria, other than direct divine communications, for deciding on rightness or wrongness. Moore turns to social considerations. He notes, for instance, that, in the society in which he lives, one of the expectations that normally arise from marriage is that the partners have exclusive sexual rights. It is also normally considered part of the love relationship that one has with one's best friend that he or she does not have an affair with one's spouse.

> The various institutions and customs of any society bind its members together in all sorts of ways, and it is in observing those institutions that justice consists, if they are themselves just institutions; and our standard for that is whether they allow people to relate to each other in a Christian way, a way in which we can live together humanly now and in the coming kingdom. It is in this sense that I mean that sexual relations are social relations, that our sexual relations involve relations not only with our present sexual partners but also with others, and they can be just and loving or unjust and unloving to those others as well as to our partners. And it is whether they are or not that is the proper criterion of whether a particular sexual activity or relation is a good one.[54]

Further on Moore points out that our bodies are loaded with significance by the society in which we live. In general, he notes, our movements and gestures do not have meaning in and of themselves, regardless of context. Indeed, the meaning of what we do with our bodies – and this includes sexual gestures – is dependent upon the context within which we act. Shared sex, however, does have a kind of natural meaning because it has a natural context. That context, he says, is a loving relationship.[55]

At the end of his book Moore refers to those who experience difficulty accepting the authority of the Church where sexual teachings are concerned and to those who reject that authority outright. He would seem to be referring mainly to the Roman Catholic Church, but the general theme, I think, could be applied further afield:

> Here the church must argue; and if I am right in my assessment of the available arguments, they are deficient. This is a serious impediment to the church's fulfilment of its commission. To those who question the church's teaching, or flatly disagree with it, it may also be a sign that that doctrine cannot be substantiated or defended and that it needs to be modified. The church needs to do more thinking about sex.[56]

That much at least is clear.

NOTES

1. Roland E. Murphy, *The Song of Songs* (Minneapolis: Fortress Press, 1990), p. 103. Murphy goes on to pose the question whether we can still give any credence to those who have heard the Song speaking of celibate love, of divine–human covenant and of spiritual as well as physical rapture. In his opinion, 'as modern expositors we should be open to the possibility that our predecessors, despite their foibles, may have caught a glimpse of theological reality that is not exhausted by the literal sense of the Song's poetry' (ibid.).

2. In this section on the Bible I have not mentioned the subject of being

rendered unclean by, for example, emission of semen or the menstrual flow. For an in-depth discussion of ritual purity/impurity, see William L. Countryman, *Dirt, Greed and Sex: Sexual Ethics in the New Testament and Their Implications for Today* (Philadelphia: Fortress Press, 1988/London: SCM Press, 1989).

3. Alastair Heron (ed.), *Towards a Quaker View of Sex* (London: Friends Home Service Committee, 1963), p. 38.

4. Derrick Sherwin Bailey, *The Man–Woman Relation in Christian Thought* (London: Longmans, 1959), p. 42.

5. Bailey writes: 'John Chrysostom, however, often more inclined to moderation in sexual questions than his western contemporaries, ventures the hesitant concession that it is possible to live with a wife and yet give heed to devotion – though he maintains that prayer is perfected through continence' (ibid., pp. 46–7).

6. *De virg.* xvii–xix.

7. *Dial.* II, 10. Translation as in *A Select Library of Nicene and Post-Nicene Fathers of the Christian Church*, vol. XI, ed. Peter Schaff and Henry Wace (Grand Rapids, Michigan: Wm B. Eerdmans, 1982), p. 43.

8. *Epist.* xxii, 20.

9. *De bono coniugali*, chs 6 and 7.

10. J. N. D. Kelly, *Jerome: His Life, Writings and Controversies* (London: Duckworth, 1975), p. 110.

11. Ibid., p. 91.

12. *Epist.* 22.

13. Op. cit., p. 103. In the letter under discussion, Jerome tells Eustochium that, when sleep overcomes her, the Bridegroom will come behind the wall, put his hand through the aperture, and touch her belly. She will then start up trembling, and will cry: 'I am wounded with love.'

14. *Epist.* 99, 2.

15. Kelly, op. cit., p. 109.

16. Bailey, op. cit., p. 49.

17. Kelly, op. cit., p. 285. Cf. Uta Ranke-Heinemann, *Eunuchs for Heaven: The Catholic Church and Sexuality* (London: André Deutsch, 1990), pp. 7–8.

18. Kelly, op. cit., note 10.

19. Ranke-Heinemann, op. cit., p. 7. She later notes: 'More recent Catholic biblical translations have restored Jerome's cuts and omitted his additions' (ibid., p. 8).

20. Tertullian, *De exhortatione castitatis*, 9.

21. Virginia Curran Hoffman, *The Codependent Church* (New York: Crossroad, 1991), p. 45.

22. Ibid., pp. 46–8.

23. *De nuptiis et concupiscentia*, i, 27.

24. John Bugge, *Virginitas: An Essay in the History of a Medieval Idea* (The Hague: Martinus Nijhoff, 1975), pp. 28–9.

25.   *De Genesi ad litteram*, 9, 5. Translation as in *Ancient Christian Writers*, no. 42, ed. Johannes Quaren *et al.* (New York: Newman Press, 1982), p. 75.

26.   Eric Fuchs, *Sexual Desire and Love: Origins and History of the Christian Ethic of Sexuality and Marriage* (Cambridge: James Clarke, 1983), pp. 107–8.

27.   John T. Noonan Jr, *Contraception: A History of Its Treatment by the Catholic Theologians and Canonists* (Cambridge, Mass.: Harvard University Press, 1965), pp. 75–6.

28.   *Summa contra gent.* iii, 124.

29.   *Summa theologiae* IIa IIae, 151, art. 3.

30.   *Summa theologiae* III (*Suppl.*), xlix, 4.

31.   Bailey, op. cit., pp. 164–5.

32.   Noonan, op. cit., p. 358. He refers to Claudius Aquaviva, letter of 24 April 1612, *Archivum romanum, Societatis Iesu*, Epp. NN 115, fol. 498. An in-depth study of Catholic tradition and recent teaching regarding parvity of matter in the sexual sphere is contained in Patrick J. Boyle, *Parvitas Materiae in Sexto in Contemporary Catholic Thought* (Lanham: University Press of America, 1987).

33.   Bailey, op. cit., pp. 181–2.

34.   Geoffrey Parrinder, *Sex in the World's Religions* (London: Sheldon Press, 1980), p. 235.

35.   See André Guindon, *The Sexual Language: An Essay in Moral Theology* (Ottawa: University of Ottawa Press, 1977), pp. 258–61, and Morton T. Kelsey and Barbara Kelsey, *Sacrament of Sexuality* (Warwick, NY: Amity House Inc., 1986), pp. 220–3.

36.   Kelsey and Kelsey, op. cit., p. 221.

37.   See ibid., p. 223. Guindon writes: 'In a survey published in 1961, R. Greenbank disclosed that nearly half the students and 20% of the faculty members at a Philadelphia medical school believed that masturbation could lead to mental illness' (op. cit., p. 261).

38.   James Nelson, *The Intimate Connection: Male Sexuality, Masculine Spirituality* (London: SPCK, 1992), pp. 26–7.

39.   *Resolutions* 41 and 43.

40.   *Resolution* 68.

41.   *Resolutions* 13 and 15.

42.   *Report* 5: *The Family in Contemporary Society*, Part 2, pp. 141ff.

43.   E. R. Norman, *Church and Society in England 1770–1970: A Historical Study* (Oxford: Clarendon Press, 1976), p. 413.

44.   Vincent J. Genovesi, *In Pursuit of Love: Catholic Morality and Human Sexuality* (Dublin: Gill & Macmillan, 1987), p. 190.

45.   John Francis Maxwell, *Slavery and the Catholic Church: The History of Catholic Teaching Concerning the Moral Legitimacy of the Institution of Slavery* (Chichester: Barry Rose Publishers, 1975), pp. 117–18.

46.   *Gaudium et spes*, 49. Translation by Austin Flannery, *Vatican Council II:*

The Conciliar and Post Conciliar Documents (Northport, NY: Costello Publishing Company, 1975).

47. Evidently, although very little seems to have been written specifically on the subject during the early centuries of the Church's history, we could add masturbation to this list.

48. Leslie D. Weatherhead, *The Mastery of Sex through Psychology and Religion* (London: Student Christian Movement Press, 1933), pp. xviii–xix.

49. William Graham Cole, *Sex and Love in the Bible* (London: Hodder & Stoughton, 1960), p. 391.

50. Regarding the specific subject of masturbation, Guindon writes: 'The change in mentality began, finally, with Freud's later clinical writings on neuroses at the end of the 19th century. But it took the Master quite a while to react against the prejudices of his time. For long he did assume in his clinical practice that all neurasthenics had first been masturbators. He even held the view that nocturnal pollutions were as damaging as masturbation was thought to be' (op. cit., p. 260).

51. See Aquinas, *Summa theologiae* Ia IIae, xxxiv, 1 ad 1.

52. Pius XI, *Ad catholici sacerdotii*, 42.

53. Gareth Moore, *The Body in Context: Sex and Catholicism* (London: SCM Press, 1992), p. 91.

54. Ibid., p. 11.

55. Ibid., p. 140.

56. Ibid., p. 213.

3

Life and Death
Issues

Christian moral teaching has tended to permit a fair amount of killing over the centuries, although, as one might expect, lines have been drawn beyond which the good Christian has been told he or she should not step. It would be quite inaccurate, however, to say that this moral teaching has remained unchanged throughout the history of Christianity. Those lines we mentioned have been redrawn from time to time. For example, teachings on and attitudes towards capital punishment within most Christian denominations are clearly very different now from those advocated within those same denominations not very long ago. Going back a little further in time, we find that some redrawing of lines had already been done in that sphere to make room for some degree of toleration for witches and heretics. In recent decades discussion about the pros and cons of abortion has resulted in calls for the lines to be redrawn yet again, and, within some branches of Christianity, that has happened, although it is not always clear where exactly the new lines are to be found. In other branches, most notably within Roman Catholicism, what has come to be called the 'traditional teaching' regarding this matter is still energetically proclaimed. In fact, regarding certain kinds of killing, the Catholic *Magisterium* claims the existence of an exceptionless moral norm. There are indeed, it proclaims, certain categories of killings which may sometimes be justified, but there are others which should never take place. Thus we find an absolute ban on direct active euthanasia, direct abortion and direct killing of oneself. Some dissatisfaction with such sweeping prohibitions has been expressed in recent times, but even many critics would be willing to admit that present Roman Catholic teaching on these matters does have the twin merits of clarity and consistency, advantages which, many would claim, are not so easily found in the teachings of many bodies outside the ranks of Roman Catholicism. Such clarity and consistency is rooted in the Catholic *Magisterium*'s more basic teaching on the killing of humans in general. Before going on to deal with the various controversies surrounding the specific subjects of abortion, suicide and euthanasia, therefore, it seems to me that we would do well to examine in some detail, and critically, received teaching on that very subject of killing in general, paying special attention to Roman Catholicism. As usual, it will be interesting to see if there is evidence of a constant, unchanging tradition.

KILLING IN GENERAL

Although it may seem self-evident to most people that killing may be permitted in cases of self-defence, not all the great Christian teachers throughout the ages have seen it that way. St Augustine, for instance, writes in one of his letters that he cannot approve of killing others in order to protect one's own life, although he does accept that a soldier or public functionary may legitimately kill someone in defending a third party or his city, if he is acting in accordance with the commission lawfully assigned to him and in a manner becoming his office.[1] In the opinion of St Ambrose, too violent self-defence should be avoided. If a man is attacked by an armed robber, he says, he should not return blow for blow, lest, in so protecting himself, he weaken the virtue of love.[2] However, according to the teaching inherited by today's Roman Catholics, if Robert is being attacked by Peter, he may use whatever force is necessary to defend himself. He may even go so far as to kill Peter if his life is in danger and no less drastic means of defence is open to him. This kind of thinking is also applied to the defence of third parties, and a somewhat more complex version of the same principle is found in just war theory. In other words, according to the received Catholic interpretation, the commandment 'Thou shalt not kill' does not necessarily have applicability when aggressors are about their business, although the proviso that defenders should use no more force than is necessary does give some protection to would-be murderers.

But what is to be done with assailants who succeed in their murderous ambitions? If we look back to the early centuries after apostolic times, we find that, although the Church was born into a world in which capital punishment was widely practised, there was no general enthusiasm for it in Christian circles. The apologist Lactantius, for example, who produced his best-known work *Divinae institutiones* ('Divine Precepts') early in the fourth century, declared himself therein to be clearly opposed to the death penalty.[3] St Augustine, on the other hand, makes the point that not all killing of human beings is sinful. Among the examples he cites of such non-sinful homicide is that of a judge or officer of the law who puts a criminal to death.[4] However, some scholars have pointed to other writings of his that would seem to indicate a certain reluctance to promote the practice. E. Vacandard, for instance, notes that he strongly denounced the infliction of the death penalty upon heretics as contrary to Christian charity, although, in that particular matter, he did move from an initial position of absolute toleration to one involving some coercion.[5] Much later, in the ninth century, Pope Nicholas I told the Bulgars that they should avoid every occasion of taking life, and, without any hesitation and in all circumstances, should save criminals as well as the innocent from death.[6] Francesco

Compagnoni notes, moreover, that, in the penitential books of the eighth and ninth centuries, capital crimes are considered only as sins:

> These, since there is always the possibility of conversion, must be expiated according to their seriousness, but never avenged by means of the death penalty. In the twelfth century, the *Decretals*, on the other hand, recognised explicitly that the State (*gladius materialis*) has the right to administer the death penalty, but that the Church (*gladius spiritualis*) has not, and that clerics may not execute it.

Compagnoni goes on to add, however, that, by this stage, 'the earlier attitude of mitigating influence on the part of the Church had disappeared, indeed for heresy and magic the Church had to watch to see that it was applied'.[7] In the following century, Aquinas took up that statement of Augustine that not all killing of humans is sinful, and referred directly to it. The Decalogue, he said, forbids only undue taking of human life. It is not an infringement of justice to execute criminals or the enemies of the state.[8] Elsewhere he adopts a tone that would shock many a modern abolitionist. Amputation is to be commended as treatment, he says, when a gangrenous limb is threatening to infect other parts of the body. In the same way, if a man is dangerous to the community and is corrupting it by some sin of his, execution is to be commended as treatment so that the common good may be preserved.[9]

Over the years, there were some dissenting voices from time to time among Anabaptists, Quakers and others, but, even after the Reformation, it seems, most Christian teachers, both Protestant and Catholic, continued to advocate the use of the death penalty when serious crime was committed. In the thirteenth century the Waldensians claimed that it was against divine law to inflict capital punishment, but in a profession of faith which he had drawn up for them in 1208, Pope Innocent III included the declaration that the secular authority can pass sentence of death without committing mortal sin, provided that it is not done from hatred, but for the vindication of good, and provided that it does not result from a hasty or inconsiderate judgement, but from one made with due solicitude.[10] As far as church leaders were concerned, the death penalty was not to be reserved only for people found guilty of murder. In 1231, for instance, Pope Gregory IX ordered that all heretics condemned by the Church should be passed over to the secular arm to receive the punishment they deserved. Although there is ample evidence to suggest a quite problematic relationship between the two men, the Emperor at the time, Frederick II, supported the Pope by enacting a law in 1237 condemning all heretics to death. In 1252, in his bull *Ad extirpanda*, Innocent IV ordered that the secular arm should use torture to extract confessions from captured heretics, and, in the same document, insisted that the secular authorities should enforce the laws against heretics within five days of their being handed over by the ecclesiastical authorities.[11] During discussions about the Inquisition, it is sometimes claimed that church authorities were not responsible for condemning to death people found guilty of heresy. This claim is often based on the fact that the execution was performed by the representatives of the state and that a plea for leniency was made by the church authorities upon handing over the unfortunate person to the secular arm. Various historians, however, have come to the conclusion that this was something of an empty gesture. Vacandard says that the casuists of the Inquisition denounced the death penalty in so many words, but, at the same time, insisted that the state enforce it:

> The formula by which they dismissed an impenitent or a relapsed heretic was thus worded: 'We dismiss you from our ecclesiastical forum, and abandon you to the secular arm. But we strongly beseech the secular court to mitigate its

sentence in such a way as to avoid bloodshed or danger of death.' We regret to state, however, that the civil judges were not supposed to take these words literally. If they were at all inclined to do so, they would have been quickly called to a sense of their duty by being excommunicated. The clause inserted by the canonists was a mere legal fiction, which did not change matters a particle.

As to why such a formula was used at all, Vacandard suggests that it was first used in other criminal cases in which passing guilty parties over to the secular arm did not imply the death penalty, and that the Inquisitors went on using it out of respect for tradition. He goes on to add that it seemed to palliate the flagrant contradiction between the teachings of Christ and this kind of ecclesiastical justice. Some Inquisitors, he notes, realized the emptiness of the formula and abandoned it altogether. They thus assumed full responsibility for the sentences imposed.[12] None of this, it seems, would have been at all upsetting to Aquinas. According to him, heretics deserve through their sin not only to be banished from the Church through excommunication, but also to be banished from this world by death. Since forgers and other malefactors are executed by the civil authorities, heretics may with much more reason be put to death. The Church, however, which seeks the conversion of the wanderer, should be merciful, he says, and should not condemn until after the first and second admonition. Then, if the heretic is still stubborn, the Church, being no longer confident about his conversion, cares for the salvation of others by excommunicating him and by handing him over to the secular court so that he may be put to death.[13]

Among the Reformed Churches, other factors sometimes played a part in 'justifying' the execution of those who were not of their particular brand of Christian persuasion. When discussing the persecution of Catholics in England, for instance, we need to take into account the fact that there was at times strong suspicion, indeed conviction, abroad that Catholics were not loyal subjects of the Crown. As for German Protestant attitudes, moreover, Martin Honecker notes that

> the reformers justified the imposition and implementation of capital punishment by the office of authority: as God's institution, civil authority has been given power to punish, the power of the sword. Luther can even make the drastic claim that it is God himself who executes, avenges and beheads when legitimate authority does so. The reformers defended the legitimacy of the death penalty for enthusiasts and Anabaptists because they regarded the rejection of the death penalty by the enthusiasts as a fundamental challenge to and denial of the power and legitimacy of secular authority.[14]

Doubtless considered the worst of heretics, witches were hunted down in a particularly ferocious manner over a lengthy period which has sometimes been described in terms of mass hysteria. This hysteria and matching persecution reached their peak in the fifteenth and sixteenth centuries. Henry Charles Lea writes of this era: 'Christendom seemed to have grown delirious, and Satan might well smile at the tribute to his power seen in the endless smoke of the holocaust which bore witness to his triumph over the Almighty. Protestant and Catholic rivalled each other in the madness of the hour.'[15] Nor was the craze confined to Europe, as is evidenced by the famous Salem witch trials in America in 1692. Some of the madness continued on into the eighteenth century. Herbert Thurston refers to the execution of a girl for witchcraft in the Protestant canton of Glarus in Switzerland in 1783.[16] The burning of heretics, witches included, however, slowly went out of fashion.[17] Not so the infliction of the death penalty for other reasons.

In 1764 the Italian scholar Cesare Beccaria published a short work on crime and punishment in which, among other things, he called for the abolition of capital punishment for most crimes. The book was soon translated into several languages, including English – an American edition appearing in 1777. It seems to have been enormously influential, but evidently did not meet with the approval of the Catholic authorities of the time, who placed it on the *Index of Forbidden Books* by decree of the Holy Office in 1766. Leandro Rossi points out that the condemnation by the Holy Office concerned the intellectual and philosophical premises from which Beccaria started. However, he adds, that does not excuse the Catholics for not having understood the signs of the times regarding capital punishment.[18] Even well into the twentieth century, many Protestant and Catholic ethicists continued to argue in favour of capital punishment, often appealing to texts from the Bible which they thought supported their claim. Various passages from the Old Testament could be cited, of course, to show that capital punishment was part of the penal code. The New Testament proved to be more problematical from the point of view of the anti-abolitionists. Indeed, Jesus' treatment of the woman taken in adultery and his Sermon on the Mount could hardly be said to provide the best of arguments in favour of punishment of any kind. A short passage in St Paul's letter to the Romans, however, was thought to do the trick. Here Paul calls for obedience to civil authority. Magistrates, he says, rather naïvely perhaps, do not bring fear to those who do good, but to those who do evil. People should live honestly and thus have the approval of authority. He then adds: 'But if you do what is wrong, then you may well be afraid; because it is not for nothing that the symbol of authority is the sword: it is there to serve God, too, as his avenger, to bring retribution to wrongdoers' (Rom 13:1–4). This was taken to mean that the state had the right to punish, even by death. Interestingly, it was often argued that, where capital punishment was concerned, there was no question of an infringement of rights. Pope Pius XII, for instance, stated in

1952 that when a condemned man is executed the state does not take away his right to life. What it does is take away the benefit of life, in expiation. The criminal has already, through his crime, deprived himself of the right to live.[19]

In a world in which many countries and numerous states of the USA have abandoned capital punishment for most (and in some cases all) crimes, some Christian leaders and ethicists continue to grant theoretical approval to the infliction of the death penalty by the state if no other suitable means of protecting society is available,[20] but, at the same time, there are others who are unwilling to grant even such theoretical approval. However, even among the members of the former group, the general feeling seems to be that, in practice, other means are almost always available. In specific cases, moreover, leaders of Christian churches have made personal appeals to governments not to administer the death penalty. After all, human experience has shown us time and again that violence has a tendency to beget violence, and, no matter how much one tries to give it a clean and respectable image, capital punishment is very clearly a premeditated act of violence. All of this is a far cry from the teachings of Aquinas and the stances taken by popes and other church leaders in bygone days.

Another category of killing that Christian ethicists have tended to justify, at least in theory, under certain conditions, is that resulting from warfare. In the early years of the Church's history, it seems, Christians on the whole were loathe to serve in the imperial armies or to take part in wars in any way whatsoever.[21] Gradually, however, attitudes changed, especially after the rise to power of the Emperor Constantine, and justifications of warfare, under certain conditions, began to appear in Christian writings. Historians of just war teaching usually trace the development of the theory from Augustine, through Aquinas and on to the modifications of Suárez and Vitoria. As it has come down to us, the theory states: (1) that there should be a just cause; (2) that war should be declared and directed only by a rightful and competent authority; (3) that it should be undertaken only as a last resort; (4) that there should be a reasonable chance of success; (5) that there should be proportionality, in the sense that the good achieved will outweigh the evil brought about; (6) that non-combatants should not be attacked directly. The last condition is concerned with conduct during war rather than with justification for declaring it in the first place. Some of the others apply to both. Another condition, which some might think should simply be taken for granted, but which is sometimes added to the list, is that there should be no ulterior, morally wrong motive for going to war.

These criteria are, of course, very general. There is therefore room for quite major disagreements among those who accept them. If we take the first condition as an example, we soon find that this has indeed been the case. Aquinas, for instance, explains the requirement of a just cause by saying that those attacked should be attacked because that is what they deserve on account of a wrong they have done. Taking up words of Augustine, he adds that we usually describe as just a war to avenge wrongs, to punish a nation or state for refusing to make amends for outrages committed by its subjects, or to restore what has been seized injuriously.[22] Several centuries later, Pius XII said that everything possible must be done to ban and proscribe the war of aggression as a legitimate means for solving international disputes.[23] There does not appear to be total agreement between these two teachers. As John Courtney Murray sees it, the Pope seems 'to be denying to individual states, in this historical moment, the *ius belli* (*compétence de guerre*) of the modern era of the unlimited sovereign state, *scil.*, the right of recourse to war, on the sovereign judgment of the national state, for the vindication of legal rights and legitimate interests'.[24] Writing some years before Aquinas, that most influential among Christians of his time, St Bernard of Clairvaux, spoke of a cause for war that few modern Christians, I imagine, would regard as just. In a letter to the English people encouraging them to take part in the Second Crusade, Bernard pointed out that God could have saved his own Holy Land by sending down legions of angels or simply by a word. Instead he feigns to put himself under the obligation of those who go to fight on his behalf so that 'in return for your taking up arms in his cause, he can reward you with pardon for your sins and everlasting glory'.[25] Clearly, some of the causes for war which were acceptable to Christian leaders and teachers of bygone days are not regarded as just causes by their present-day counterparts, but those present-day counterparts have disagreements among themselves. Some claim to be totally pacifist. Others would find just cause for war only in the need to protect lives. Then there are others who speak of lack of freedom as a just cause, but, of course, the word 'freedom' has many nuances, so we must expect disagreement even within this sub-category. Furthermore, nowadays, more than in earlier times, it would seem, the need for proportionality has its effect upon deliberations about what constitutes a just cause because of the terrible weapons that would be used in any war that erupted, especially between well-armed nations.

On the subject of war being undertaken only by legitimate authority, Michael K. Duffey writes:

Before Vatican II, the Catholic Church held that governments were primarily responsible for decisions regarding the use of military force. While acknowledging that citizen-soldiers bore responsibility for their personal conduct in war, the church counselled citizens that they should comply with the commands of the state. Hence, when Austrian Catholic Franz Jägerstätter refused conscription into the army of the Third Reich because of his conviction that Hitler's war was unjust, his position found no ecclesiastical support. In fact, his local bishop discouraged him from concerning himself with the moral issue of the justice of Hitler's war, urging Jägerstätter to leave moral accountability for the war to the relevant political authorities and to consider instead his primary obligation to the welfare of his family. Two decades later Pope Pius XII, in his 1956 Christmas message, condemned wars of aggression but affirmed that in a war of legitimate national defense a Catholic could not 'make appeal to his conscience as ground for refusing to give his services'.[26]

Duffey goes on to say, however, that a different position is reflected in a document of the Second Vatican Council. In *Gaudium et spes*, he notes, 'the bishops affirmed the right of individuals to abide by their consciences in matters of the use of military force and urged nations to make "humane provision for the case of those who, for reasons of conscience, refuse to bear arms" '.[27]

Having thus discussed the question of the rightness or wrongness of killing those who are 'not innocent', and having found neither constant and unchanging tradition over the centuries nor total agreement even today, we must now turn to the subject of killing people who are clearly not guilty of aggression or of anything else that Christian teachers over the ages have considered might merit the death penalty. Here Catholic ethicists especially have claimed to have a clear and unchanging teaching. Provided that there is sufficient reason, they say, even people such as these may be killed. In this case, however, the killing must be brought about in an indirect way. This can happen, for instance, in warfare. Let us suppose that a necessary bombardment of an enemy installation would cause the deaths of some non-combatants. Provided that they are not intended as the end or aim of the bombardment and provided they are not the means by which the good which is being sought is brought about, those deaths may be justified as tragic, but unintended, side effects.

Having made the above exceptions, we arrive at a norm which, we are told, does not permit of any further exceptions:

'no direct killing of innocents or of oneself'. This use of the word 'innocents', not surprisingly, has been known to cause some difficulties. It does not, of course, mean that the people involved have never done anything wrong. In current literature it is sometimes translated as 'non-aggressors'. That may or may not be an apt translation for today, but, as we have seen, it would have been a quite misleading one at times in the past. Some of the victims of 'justified' capital punishment were clearly not guilty of aggression. Whatever may be the meaning that we should assign to that particular word 'innocent', the norm has been said by numerous writers, Catholic and otherwise, to come from God. Only the Lord of life and death, we hear it said, has the right to decide when a person should die. Apparently, God allows the exceptions described above involving indirect killing of non-aggressors and even direct killing of those guilty of aggression or anything else that renders one 'not innocent'. However, it has to be said that it is not at all clear how God has communicated his/her thinking regarding these exceptions. It is worth pointing out, moreover, that appeals to the will of God in moral matters tend to be somewhat selective. Take, for instance, God's explicit command to Saul: 'Now, go and crush Amalek; put him under the curse of destruction with all that he possesses. Do not spare him, but kill man and woman, babe and suckling, ox and sheep, camel and donkey' (1 Sam 15:3). Regarding this case, says Rudolf Ginters, we would undoubtedly say that God cannot have commanded such a thing. The story has to be interpreted differently. He then turns to the New Testament, where he finds what he calls a docile acceptance of the juridical institution of slavery and a call for women to submit to their husbands. We should not interpret what is expressed in these cases as moral demands coming from God, he says.[28] We would, I imagine, all agree, but only because we do not believe that God could command what is morally wrong. Such a stand, however, presupposes that we can have knowledge about what is morally good or right before God tells us. That is precisely Ginters's point. Appealing to the will of God to resolve moral problems, he says, is unacceptable.[29] It would seem, then, that, rather than say that certain actions are right or wrong because God commands or forbids them, we should merely say that God calls upon us to do what is right and avoid what is wrong. However, we often have to use various tools – including the accumulated wisdom of humankind, our own moral sensitivities and our reasoning powers – to find out precisely what is right and wrong in particular situations.

The theological or divine sovereignty argument against killing is not always expressed in terms of commands and exceptions expressly made by God. Instead, notes Ginters, we hear it said that, for wise and just reasons, God has deprived humans of the right to formulate judgements regarding such matters. In this case too, as Ginters again notes, we run into the problem of precisely how we know what God has decided. Furthermore, if we say that God has created every human and, therefore, only God can take a human's life, we run the risk of reducing the relationship between Creator and creature to the level of one between creatures, involving competition over rights. From the ethical point of view, continues Ginters, nothing emerges from the fact that God is the Creator of life. This theological argument, and others like it, are simply pseudo-arguments.[30]

Josef Fuchs has also confronted the divine sovereignty argument. Humans, he says, have been made lords of themselves, while God's lordship is transcendent. We should not see ourselves as mere managers or administrators of what God owns. It is also incorrect, he says, to talk about divine 'authorization' or 'delegation' whenever the human disposal of human life is approved. If the human person is constituted by God to be a dialogical and co-operative partner (and, therefore, lord in this world), neither that kind of talk nor references to God's law and rights are well grounded. Human authority, he continues, does not become true authority because God gives a binding character to human decrees. We can say, rather, that it is

> a created participation in God's transcendent authority. Similarly, the human search and discovery of morally right conduct and action in this world have the character of moral norms because of the fact that God has established the earthly lordship of human persons, certainly not only with regard to some universal laws, but also through their *insights* which go into detail and hence are very differentiated.[31]

It would seem, therefore, that, where killing of oneself or innocent people is concerned, we have to apply our moral sensitivities and our powers of moral reasoning just as we do in other areas of ethics. It could be claimed, of course, that sound moral reasoning points to a complete ban on direct killing of oneself and non-aggressors. In recent years, however, discussion of certain cases of therapeutic abortion and self-killing has caused some doubt to be expressed regarding the validity of such a claim.

Bearing in mind what we have just discussed regarding killing in general, let us, then, turn to the more specific and, for many people, controversial issues of abortion, suicide and euthanasia.

ABORTION

One of the cases most discussed under this heading in recent times has been that of ectopic pregnancy where the embryo is forming in a Fallopian tube. The embryo will virtually inevitably die eventually, and so too will the woman unless a surgical intervention is made. In the recent past such cases were resolved in Roman Catholic circles, apparently without too much controversy, by having recourse to a 'traditional' device known as the principle of double effect. Now, according to this principle, one is justified in performing an action which has both good and bad effects if, and only if, all four of the following conditions are fulfilled: (1) The action is in itself good or at least indifferent. It is not morally wrong. (2) The intention of the person acting is good. He or she does not intend the evil effect. (The word 'intention' here refers to the reason for the performance of the act.) (3) The good accomplished is at least as immediate as the evil. The evil effect must not be the means of bringing about the good. (4) There must be a proportionately grave reason for allowing the evil to come about.

In a case of ectopic pregnancy such as that described above, until complications arose in recent times, it was held that, provided the Fallopian tube could be classified as pathological, the action of removing it (with the embryo inside) could be described as the excision of that tube.[32] The first condition would thus be fulfilled. The demands of the second condition would also be met because the doctor's intention is that of saving the woman's life. The third condition is fulfilled because the woman's life is saved by the removal of the tube and not by means of the death of the embryo. Finally, the woman's life being at stake provides the proportionate reason.

In recent years, however, developments in medical science, and the likelihood of further developments, have produced complications and new questions. For example, what if the woman's life could be saved by removing the embryo without excising the tube? This possibility has led some to say that, at least in this case, direct killing of an innocent person can be justified, provided, of course, that the lives of both mother and embryo could not be saved by somehow moving the embryo to the uterus and inducing it to implant therein. The removal (and therefore the killing) of the embryo is what is immediately brought about by the surgeon's action, and the good of saving the woman's life is dependent upon that removal of the embryo. According to some commentators, such a killing would be direct. However, there are others who try to retain the 'indirect' label in such cases. Germain Grisez is one of these, but accepts that the usual modern formulation of the principle of double effect is too restrictive because it demands that the evil aspect of the act not precede the good even in the order of physical causality. Regarding the removal of the embryo in a case of ectopic pregnancy such as the one described above, he writes:

> The embryo's death is not a means and is in no way helpful to solving the problem. Rather, one can make this choice – to remove the ectopic embryo – simply to remove its threat to the mother's life, accepting the embryonic child's certain death only as an inevitable side effect.[33]

In order to get a clear understanding of his position it is important to note that Grisez admits that the removal of the embryo is necessary if the woman's life is to be saved. The embryo's death, however, is not necessary for that end. It just so happens that, given the present state of medical and biological science, such removal will inevitably result in the embryo's death. Grisez has undoubtedly made a fine attempt to preserve the direct/indirect distinction. Some years ago, however, Paul Ramsey wrote:

> I have in mind the repeatable (if rare) case of a pregnant woman who has a misplaced, acute appendicitis and who will die from its rupture unless a physician goes straight through the uterus (i.e., kills the baby first, then saves her life). Also, there are cases of aneurysm of the aorta in which the wall of the aorta is so weakened that it balloons out behind the pregnant uterus. Again the physician must first kill the fetus in order to deal with the aneurysm that threatens the mother's life.[34]

When he wrote this piece, Ramsey was of the opinion that Grisez would probably not justify abortion in such cases. Whatever may or may not be the truth of that, the fact remains that these are difficult test cases for members of a tradition which opposes direct killing of non-aggressors. Let us suppose, however, that, in these cases, there is no possibility that the foetuses will survive with or without surgery. How many of us are convinced that letting the women die would be a fully human response?

Joyce Poole adds other complications to the subject of ectopic pregnancies. First she points out that the tube is a 'diseased organ' only in the sense that it is being distended by the embryo which it contains. She accepts that, if left alone, in almost all cases the tube will rupture and cause serious haemorrhage. 'Cases have been reported, however, of the diagnosis having been missed and of the pregnancy continuing in the abdominal cavity with the placenta attaching itself to internal organs. A live baby has been delivered at term by Caesarean section, after this so-called "abdominal pregnancy".' Poole then goes on to describe such a case from her own experience as a physician, and asks:

> Could there be a moral case, therefore, for leaving an ectopic pregnancy alone on the slight chance that it might be that very occasional one which survives? If the 8-week embryo really has the same rights as the mother the answer would surely have to be yes. It would certainly develop at grave risk to maternal safety, but so does the one whose mother is in renal failure.
>
> Once again it would seem that attempts to apply absolute rules to particular cases lead not only to impossible medical dilemmas but to philosophical muddles.[35]

It may be objected that cases in which such pregnancies success-fully come to term are extremely rare. That may well be so, but the fact remains that, if Catholic teaching allows abortions in such cases, things are not quite as they may have seemed. Even if we ignore the controversy surrounding the possibility of removing the embryo without excising the tube, we need to bear in mind the fact that it has become common not to wait for the tube to rupture before removing it, it being argued that the tube is diseased through the embryo's presence there. In short, we can say that abortions are allowed in such cases because of a serious risk to the mother's life, in spite of the fact that there is an admittedly very slim chance that the pregnancy will come to term successfully.

The subject of abortion is also sometimes discussed in association with rape. Regarding the permissible time frame within which attempts may be made to prevent or stop pregnancy resulting from rape, Philip S. Keane wrote some years ago:

> Traditional Roman Catholic theology allowed efforts to remove the semen to go on for quite a number of hours after rape, even though fertilization may take place within thirty minutes of intercourse. Past theologians took this position because in the light of the great evil of rape they wanted to give raped women the benefit of the doubt as long as there was any reasonable probability that fertilization had not taken place. In other words, our theology always used a 'benefit of reasonable doubt model' when dealing with the victims of rape.[36]

Even within the ranks of Roman Catholicism, there are theologians who have begun to cast doubt upon the personhood of the embryo during the early days of pregnancy. However, while acknowledging the lack of certainty about the beginning of personhood, the Catholic *Magisterium* has held in recent documents that the human embryo must be treated as a person from the moment of conception[37] (notwithstanding the fact that various commentators have pointed out that 'moment' is a misleading word when applied to the process of fertilization).

Given this stance, the above description of the treatment of rape victims appears all the more surprising. Some may react by saying that, given the horror of rape, it is eminently reasonable, but the fact remains that exceptions made for rape victims are still exceptions. In other words, if any exception at all is made to what has been dubbed an exceptionless norm, that norm simply ceases to be exceptionless. Why is the benefit of doubt made to weigh in favour of the rape victim and not in favour of an embryo that might be present? Do the arguments in favour of the girl or woman weigh more heavily than those in favour of such an embryo? I imagine that very few, if any, people in the Catholic Church, even at the hierarchical level, would be inclined to call for a less favourable attitude towards the victims of rape, but it would be interesting to hear their precise reasons for taking such a stance.

There has been a good deal of discussion in recent times about what to do when a victim of rape is known to be pregnant and does not wish to continue with the pregnancy. Surely most people, Catholic and otherwise, who take the view that direct killing of the innocent is in general wrong would have some sympathy with Bernard Häring's comments regarding the pastoral counselling of such a person: 'I would not pursue the question once it had become evident that the woman could not bear the burden of the pregnancy.'[38] While we could quite legitimately claim, as Häring does, that the decision is the woman's, it seems to me that something else is involved in such a stance. One sees that the burden is intolerable for this person and, for that very reason, decides not to put pressure on her to do something that is just too much for her. Those who speak in terms of weighing values might say that, in this case, we have found a good enough or sufficiently important reason (a proportionate reason, if you like) for at least tolerating a direct abortion.

SUICIDE

Another area of controversy is suicide. Having discussed the significance of God's sovereignty where suicide is concerned, Adrian Holderegger concludes that a judgement about the moral rightness or wrongness of it can be obtained only by comparing conflicting values or evils:

> As we have explained, man's status as a creature and his claim to freedom that are implied by God's sovereignty only provide a 'grammar' for treating life responsibly rather than arbitrarily. They include the imperative to translate the reality of creation into action in a responsible manner. In this man recognises himself as something entrusted to himself and called to give himself and reality a humane meaning. Among theologians this fundamental insight has increasingly given rise to the conviction that there is no other way than establishing the possibility of killing or suicide as one given by the creator along with the actual power of running one's own life, so as to conclude that man has to make the moral judgment of the circumstances in which it is to be regarded as justified and in which it is not. On these presuppositions suicide cannot be regarded *a priori* as an action evil in itself (*malum in se*) independent of the circumstances and consequences: the fact of human responsibility leaves open the real possibility of suicide for morally responsible reasons, even if in actual fact it has yet to be determined whether a case of direct suicide can exist as a responsible deed.[39]

In recent years there has been a fair amount of discussion about a hypothetical case involving the self-killing of a secret agent who is captured by enemy soldiers. He has information which, in the hands of those same enemy soldiers, would spell disaster for his people. Being as certain as he can be that, through a combination of torture, drugs and various brainwashing techniques, the soldiers will eventually get the information out of him, he kills himself. Numerous scholars have suggested that the agent would be justified in doing so if there were no other way in which he could reasonably be expected to keep the information away from the enemy. The present writer has yet to hear convincing arguments to the contrary, and yet this person's death would clearly not be a mere side effect. It would be necessary for the protection of his people. The killing would therefore be direct. It would seem, then, that, if we are right in justifying this particular act of self-killing, the norm forbidding direct killing of oneself and non-aggressors is not exceptionless.

Now, let us suppose that the secret agent needs help, and that one of his own side has infiltrated the enemy ranks. The infiltrator assists his suicide by secretly bringing a small pouch containing poison into his prison cell. The agent then puts this poison into his food or drink. If one accepts that the self-killing is justified, there seems to be no reason for condemning the assistance given by another party who, like the secret agent, is convinced that, unless the agent dies, the enemy will get and use the information which he is carrying in his head. To complete the scenario, let us assume that, even with the help of the infiltrator, escape is out of the question.

Such mention of assisted suicide would seem to lead us quite logically to the subject of euthanasia, but, before going on to discuss that subject, we would do well to reflect a little. What we have done so far is to question the validity of the teaching that self-killing and direct killing of non-aggressors can never be justified. If there are indeed exceptions to that norm – and the above discussion would seem to indicate that there may be – the exceptionless norm prohibiting direct euthanasia loses its traditional basis. It does not necessarily follow that euthanasia may sometimes be justified. However, anybody attempting to formulate an exceptionless ban on it would need, it seems, to find a new basis for that ban.

EUTHANASIA

Specific mention of the direct/indirect distinction is sometimes encountered in traditional Catholic teaching concerning euthanasia. Thus we find health-care professionals being told that they may administer pain-killing drugs to terminally ill patients who are suffering great pain and who request such treatment, even though those same drugs will have the side effect of shortening the patients' lives. There is, however, another distinction which has acquired importance in debates about euthanasia and which, especially in Roman Catholic circles, has become part of 'traditional' teaching on the subject. It is the distinction between active and passive euthanasia, between killing and letting die. It may be thought by some that it is obvious that killing is necessarily worse than merely allowing people to die, but is it? James Rachels faces up to this question by considering two cases:

> In the first, Smith stands to gain a large inheritance if anything should happen to his six-year-old cousin. One evening while the child is taking his bath, Smith sneaks into the bathroom and drowns the child, and then arranges things so that it will look like an accident.
>
> In the second, Jones also stands to gain if anything should happen to his six-year-old cousin. Like Smith, Jones sneaks in planning to drown the child in his bath. However, just as he enters the bathroom Jones sees the child slip and hit his head, and fall face down in the water. Jones is delighted; he stands by, ready to push the child's head back under if it is necessary, but it is not necessary. With only a little thrashing about, the child drowns all by himself, 'accidentally', as Jones watches and does nothing.

It would be accurate to say that, in the first case, Smith kills the child, whereas, in the second, Jones merely lets the child die. If letting die were in itself less bad than killing, the fact that Jones did not kill the boy might be expected to carry some weight. 'But', notes Rachels, 'it does not. Such a "defense" can only be regarded as a grotesque perversion of moral reasoning. Morally speaking, it is no defense at all.'[40] It could be said, of course, that we have problems with the motivation here. However, it should be pointed out that the motivation is the same in both cases. The only significant difference between them is that between killing and letting die. Now, suppose we take two cases in which the common motivation is one with which we can empathize. Let us imagine that two doctors wish to spare their terminally ill patients terrible suffering. One merely withholds or ceases treatment. The other injects a lethal dose. Does the distinction between killing and letting die become significant in such cases because the motivation is more palatable? That would be the case if the divine sovereignty argument were valid, because then we could say that it is good to spare the patient suffering, but only God has the right to do so by taking life. We have already seen that, when examined, this theological argument is far from convincing, but are there more weighty reasons for upholding the distinction between killing and letting die?

In an article published a few years ago, Josef Fuchs considered the problem of the certainly irreversible coma:

> If one gives a positive answer in such situations to the controversial question of whether the justified act of letting a person die and active euthanasia are to be judged as equivalent and therefore morally similar, one must still bear in mind that the justified act of letting a person die, as an expressive attitude, stands nearer to an attitude expressing respect vis-à-vis human life than does an active intervention.[41]

This argument most certainly needs to be taken into account when considering whether or not direct active euthanasia can ever be justified. There are, moreover, a number of other arguments against permitting direct euthanasia. Kevin Kelly listed four which are far from negligible in an article published over twenty years ago. The first of these is the danger of escalation. Whether or not there is such a danger depends on the basic approach of those who are in favour of euthanasia:

> For instance, many supporters of voluntary euthanasia base their case on respect for the freedom of the individual human being, but it may well be that their understanding of who qualifies for the category of 'human being' depends on the quality of human life present. If this were so, it would be logical for them to regard the state as an institution to safeguard and promote the common good of 'good quality human beings'.

The second argument is that there is a danger that, in some cases, the consent of the patient to euthanasia will not really be free. An old person, for instance, who is suffering from an incurable terminal disease might feel a kind of moral obligation to request euthanasia in order to relieve the burden imposed on relatives. The third point, and a far from insignificant one, is the possibility of bad effects upon the medical profession. There might be a reduction in reverence for human life, and confidence in the single-mindedness of the profession could be destroyed. Furthermore, there could be a bad effect upon medical progress if euthanasia were regarded as an acceptable solution to medical problems. The fourth argument listed by Kelly concerns the possibility of a harmful effect upon society. As long as human dignity is not based simply on usefulness to society, he says, such people as the mentally ill, the severely handicapped, the very young and the incurably sick must be treated with respect and their lives safeguarded. An acceptance even of voluntary euthanasia 'would seem to involve a weakening of this basic position'.[42]

These are indeed weighty arguments, and they could well lead us to conclude that active euthanasia should be justified only in rare and exceptional circumstances. To say that, however, is very different from saying that it could never be justified. Arguments very similar to all of the above (with the exception of the one referring to the danger of the lack of free consent) have been and are advanced as reasons why we should not tell lies or break promises. There was a time, indeed a very long period of time, when it was generally taught in Christian circles that one should never tell an untruth even to save the life of one's neighbour. Common sense and homicidal maniacs have contributed to a change of attitude in that regard. Few now, I imagine, would oppose a teaching that the telling of untruths may sometimes be justified.[43] The same holds for the breaking of promises. It would seem, therefore, that, at least on a theoretical level, we cannot rule out the possibility that direct active euthanasia might, in exceptional cases, be justified. There is still that argument about the danger of the lack of free consent. Even without entering into a discussion about ways of overcoming this problem, however, surely we would all agree that this argument cannot be the basis for an exceptionless norm. It is perhaps also worth noting that all of the points raised by Kelly could be used as arguments against allowing doctors to withdraw or withhold treatment from terminally ill patients. In other words, they could be used as arguments against passive as well as active euthanasia. They could, moreover, be used well in such a role because there is evidence that, in recent times, there has been some misuse of the permission granted in most countries to 'let patients die'.

To achieve greater clarity regarding the rights and wrongs of active euthanasia, it might be useful to draw a parallel with the case referred to above of the secret agent whose self-killing is assisted by the infiltrator from his own side. Compare that with the case of a soldier who has to leave his horribly wounded friend on the battlefield because his unit is retreating. He knows, not only that his friend will suffer an excruciatingly painful death, but that the enemy soldiers from whom his unit is retreating are sadistic and delight in tormenting wounded soldiers from the other side. His friend has asked him to kill him. As an expression of love and respect, he does so. This would be a case of voluntary euthanasia. Could it be justified? If not, why not?

Similar questions arise concerning euthanasia in the world of health care. The majority view of an Institute of Medical Ethics working party in Great Britain has been formulated as follows:

> A doctor, acting in good conscience, is ethically justified in assisting death if the need to relieve intense and unceasing pain or distress caused by an incurable illness greatly out-weighs the benefit to the patient of further prolonging his life. This conclusion applies to patients whose sustained wishes on this matter are known to the doctor and should thus be respected as outweighing any contrary opinions expressed by others. Assistance of death, however, is not justified until the doctor and the clinical team are sure that the patient's pain and distress cannot be relieved by any other means – pharmacological, surgical, psychological, or social. To this end the views of medical and other professional colleagues and of the patient's family must be ascertained as fully as is consistent with maintenance of the patient's trust.[44]

Perhaps, when discussing euthanasia, we have tended to con-centrate too much upon the value of life and have given too little consideration to persons and relationships. After all, there is general agreement in Christian circles that life is a fundamental value but not an absolute one. Could we not say that it is at least theoretically possible that care for a particular person in a particular situation might be best expressed by helping that person to die? A greater emphasis on relationships may help overcome the danger of abuse. A glimpse at the biblical tradition concerning justice may be of help here. As John R. Donahue puts it, 'In general terms the biblical idea of justice can be described as *fidelity to the demands of a relationship*'.[45] If emphasis is put on the demands of the doctor–patient relationship, it seems to me that there is less chance of our sliding towards the far from negligible dangers highlighted by Kelly. Fuchs's point about expressive attitudes would also be catered for. We can surely contemplate the possibility that, in meeting the demands of the doctor–patient relationship by helping the patient to die, a physician may be expressing something entirely positive. Lisa Cahill says something not entirely unlike this:

> On the whole, Christian tradition envisions life as a fundamental value but not an absolute one. This is why causing death can be a form of respect for life, and particularly for the total dignity and welfare of persons, which include spiritual as well as physical aspects. This same tradition has limited causation to indirect means although that limit is the subject of ongoing discussion among those who see relief of suffering as a duty of love which can in exceptional cases outweigh the stringent duty not to destroy life directly.[46]

It might be pointed out here, however, that one argument from Christian tradition has not been dealt with sufficiently. The divine sovereignty argument may have been disposed of, but there is the other theological notion of life as a gift from God. In response, I would venture to suggest that it is possible for someone to respect life as a divine gift, indeed, as a gift with a purpose, and yet to cause death without losing any of that respect for life, or, indeed, for God. After all, if the giftedness of life meant that we should not make any decisions regarding its continued existence in this earthly dimension, we would be wrong to deliberately put our lives at risk for what we see to be a good enough reason.

Having said all of this, there is still need to emphasize the fact that one must proceed with extreme caution in this sphere of human activity. In his article referred to above, the arguments which I have taken up were presented by Kelly as reasons for opposing permissive euthanasia *legislation*. As such, they are very strong arguments indeed, and one can well understand why, in certain parts of the world, although a more permissive attitude towards extreme cases has developed in recent times, there have been no changes in the law banning euthanasia. There is merely a certain toleration in some places and what we might call the 'turning of a blind eye' in others. This is undoubtedly a most untidy situation and, in many ways, an undesirable one. Nevertheless, even in the event of our all being convinced that there are (probably very rare) cases in which assisted death should be permitted, it is difficult to see how thoroughly satisfactory changes in law could be effected without running into the problems listed by Kelly.

It will, perhaps, have been noted that we have, in effect, discussed only the possibility of justifying *voluntary* euthanasia. Some people may feel that the same arguments could be used to justify the *involuntary* kind. We should point out, however, that Fuchs's argument and three of Kelly's would take on much greater weight in such circumstances. Furthermore, Kelly's remaining argument about the danger of the lack of free consent would, of course, need to be outweighed before any discussion of the matter could even begin.

CONCLUDING REMARKS

As is the case in so many other areas of moral theology, claims about constant and unchanging teachings regarding the rights and wrongs of killing human beings are clearly not based on

historical facts. In this chapter we have seen considerable variations. It might be claimed that now we have arrived at a point
where, at least as far as the Roman Catholic *Magisterium* is concerned, we have a clear teaching that, provided there is sufficient reason, direct killing is permitted only in the case of
aggressors. Otherwise only indirect killing is permitted, and
again only if there is sufficient reason. This, it might be said,
is what is meant by 'no direct killing of the innocent'. The word
'innocent' may not have meant only 'non-aggressor' in the not
too distant past, but, it might be insisted, that is clearly the
meaning intended now. Such claims may be made, but we have
seen that there are some reasons for thinking that, while this
norm may be a good general guideline which applies in the vast
majority of cases, there may be some exceptions.

It goes without saying that we must have very good reasons
indeed for any kind of killing of our fellow humans. That applies
even to the killing of aggressors. The chances are, moreover,
that the ending of terrible suffering will not be sufficient reason
in most cases to justify direct active voluntary euthanasia because
of the applicability of those arguments we extracted from the
writings of Fuchs and Kelly. It would seem, however, that
the dictates of neither God nor sound moral reasoning can be
appealed to as the basis for an *exceptionless* norm banning all self-
killing and direct killing of non-aggressors. Nevertheless, whatever we may think about the various changes in teaching which
took place over the centuries, the wisdom we have received from
our ancestors regarding life and death issues would appear to
be much more highly developed than is the case with some of
the other matters discussed in this book. Although in the history
of Christianity there have been some disastrous episodes along
the way (e.g., 'holy wars', and the burning of heretics and
witches), we can see that, albeit slowly, there has been the
development of norms which have arisen from a deep and
highly developed sensitivity towards the value of human life.
Furthermore, while some of what has been said in this chapter

might seem to cast doubt upon the existence of a truly exceptionless norm regarding the killing of non-aggressors and
oneself, it seems to me that, in practice, any change regarding
the taking of human life should be only very slight indeed.
Nevertheless, it could be said that a shift towards what is best
for the person and away from mere principles concerning the
preservation of life, in the purely biological sense, would involve
a significant change in attitude.

NOTES

1. St Augustine, *Epist.* 47. See also *De libero arbitrio*, I, v.
2. St Ambrose, *On the Duties of the Clergy*, 3.4.27.
3. Lactantius, *Divinae institutiones*, VI, 20.
4. St Augustine, *De libero arbitrio*, I, iv.
5. E. Vacandard, *The Inquisition: A Critical and Historical Study of the Coercive Power of the Church* (New York: Longmans, Green & Co., 1908), pp. 12–22.
6. Nicholas I, *Epist.* 97.
7. Francesco Compagnoni, 'Capital punishment and torture in the tradition of the Roman Catholic Church', *Concilium* 120 (1979), p. 48.
8. Thomas Aquinas, *Summa theologiae* Ia IIae, q. 100, art. 8, ad 3.
9. Ibid., IIa IIae, q. 64, art. 2.
10. Denzinger (32nd edn, 1963), 795.
11. For a fuller discussion, see Vacandard, op. cit., pp. 105ff.
12. Vacandard, op. cit., pp. 178–80.
13. Thomas Aquinas, *Summa theologiae*, IIa IIae, q. 11, art. 3. Vacandard writes: 'St Thomas defended the death penalty without indicating how it was to be inflicted. The commentators who followed him were more definite. The *Animadversio debita*, says Henry of Susa (Hostiensis; †1271), in his commentary on the bull *Ad abolendam*, is the penalty of the stake (*ignis crematio*). He defends this interpretation by quoting the words of Christ: "If any one abide not in me, he shall be cast forth as a branch, and shall wither, and they shall gather him *and cast him into the fire*, and he *burneth*." Jean d'Andre (†1348), whose commentary carried equal weight with Henry of Susa's throughout the Middle Ages, quotes the same text as authority for sending heretics to the stake. According to this peculiar exegesis, the law and custom of the day merely sanctioned the law of Christ' (op. cit., pp. 176–7).
14. Martin Honecker, 'Capital punishment in German Protestant theology', *Concilium* 120 (1979), p. 55.

15.   Henry Charles Lea, *A History of the Inquisition of the Middle Ages* (London: Sampson Low, Marston, Searle & Rivington, 1888), vol. 3, p. 549.

16.   Herbert Thurston, 'Witchcraft' in *The Catholic Encyclopedia* (New York: The Robert Appleton Company, 1912), vol. 15, p. 677.

17.   Some are of the opinion that a change in attitudes towards sex may have played a part in bringing the lunacy to an end. Charles Berg notes that 'it might be assumed that the cessation of such a fantastic procedure as the torture and burning of women for fornication with the devil must have been the product of a saner psychology. After a profound study of the subject, Ernest Jones came to a very different conclusion: "The end of the Witch epidemic needs almost as much explanation as its origin . . . There was a notable increase in Puritanism . . . the general attitude towards sex and sexuality underwent a very extensive change. Instead of its being loudly declaimed and stamped on as a dangerous sin, it became more and more suppressed as a topic of public discussion . . . Now this change of attitude was quite inconsistent with a continuance of the Witch epidemic, for the Witch trials consisted largely of ventilating in great detail the most repellant aspects of sexuality" ' (*Fear, Punishment, Anxiety and the Wolfenden Report* (London: George Allen & Unwin, 1959), pp. 57–8.

18.   Leandro Rossi, 'Pena di morte (ed ergastolo)' in *Dizionario enciclopedico di teologia morale*, ed. L. Rossi and A. Valsecchi (Rome: Edizioni Paoline, 1976), p. 749.

19.   Pius XII, Address to the First International Congress of the Histopathology of the Nervous System, 14 September 1952: *AAS*, vol. 45, p. 787.

20.   Such is the stance taken in the *Catechism of the Catholic Church*, paras 2263–2267 (*Catéchisme de l'Église Catholique* (Mame/Plon 1992), pp. 463–4).

21.   Louis J. Swift writes: 'If it is presumptuous to say that there were two traditions in the period before Constantine, it is at least clear that there were two sides to the issue. The most vocal and the most articulate side was pacifist. In this school Tertullian, Origen and the early Lactantius stand out as the most reflective and persuasive writers. Although they do not all agree on the reasons for opposing Christian participation in war or military service, although they are not of one mind on the amount of cooperation they will allow a Christian in such matters, and although they are not always consistent in their own thinking on the subject, they leave no doubt that for them violence of any kind is incompatible with the demands of the Christian faith.

    'The other side is non-pacifist. It has no apologists that we know of, and no articulated rationale. Both the fact of its existence and the arguments on which it is based are gleaned indirectly from a very few sources' (*The Early Fathers on War and Military Service* (Wilmington, Delaware: Michael Glazier, 1983), pp. 27–8).

22. Thomas Aquinas, *Summa theologiae* IIa IIae, q. 40, art. 1.

23. Pius XII, Christmas Message, 1944: *AAS*, 37 (1945), p. 18.

24. John Courtney Murray, 'Remarks on the moral problem of war', *Theological Studies* 20 (1959), p. 46.

25. *Epist.* 391. Translation in *The Letters of Saint Bernard of Clairvaux* (London: Burns & Oates, 1953), pp. 460–3.

26. Michael K. Duffey. 'The just war teaching: From Tonkin Gulf to Persian Gulf', *America* (2 February 1991), pp. 83–4.

27. Ibid., p. 84.

28. Rudolf Ginters, *Valori, norme e fede cristiana* (Casale Monferrato: Marietti, 1982), pp. 34–5. This is the Italian translation of *Werte und Normen: Einführung in die philosophische und theologische Ethik.*

29. Ibid., p. 35.

30. Ibid., pp. 35–7.

31. Josef Fuchs, *Christian Morality: The Word Becomes Flesh* (Washington DC: Georgetown University Press, 1987), pp. 47–8.

32. Clearly mutilation of the woman's body, which is what the excision of the tube amounts to, is itself a bad effect. So-called 'traditionalist' Catholic moral theologians, however, tend to make use of the principle of totality to justify surgical operations. According to this principle, a part of the organism may be sacrificed for the good of the whole. The presence of an embryo or foetus renders this principle insufficient. Hence the use of the principle of double effect to deal with cases involving ectopic pregnancies.

33. G. Grisez, *Christian Moral Principles*, vol. 1 of *The Way of the Lord Jesus* (Chicago: Franciscan Herald Press, 1983), pp. 298–9.

34. Paul Ramsey, 'Abortion: A review article', *The Thomist* 37 (1973), p. 214.

35. Joyce Poole, *The Cross of Unknowing: Dilemmas of a Catholic Doctor* (London: Sheed & Ward, 1989), pp. 47–8.

36. Philip S. Keane, *Sexual Morality: A Catholic Perspective* (New York: Paulist Press, 1977), p. 137.

37. See, for instance, Congregation for the Doctrine of the Faith, *Instruction on Respect for Human Life in Its Origin and on the Dignity of Procreation: Replies to Certain Questions of the Day* (1987).

38. Bernard Häring, *Medical Ethics* (Slough: St Paul Publications, 1991), p. 106.

39. Adrian Holderegger, 'A right to a freely chosen death? Some theological considerations', *Concilium* 179 (1985), pp. 94–5.

40. James Rachels, 'Active and passive euthanasia' in *Killing and Letting Die*, ed. Bonnie Steinbock (Englewood Cliffs, NJ: Prentice-Hall, 1980), pp. 65–6.

41. Fuchs, *Christian Morality*, p. 79. See also Ginters, op. cit., p. 40.

42. Kevin Kelly, 'Why should Catholics oppose euthanasia legislation?', *Catholic Gazette* (April 1970), pp. 5–6.

43. See, however, Germain Grisez, *The Way of the Lord Jesus*, vol. 2: *Living a Christian Life* (Quincy, Illinois: Franciscan Press, 1993), pp. 406–7.

44. Institute of Medical Ethics Working Party on the Ethics of Prolonging Life and Assisting Death, 'Assisted death', *The Lancet* (8 September 1990), p. 613.

45. John R. Donahue, 'Biblical perspectives on justice', *The Faith That Does Justice: Examining the Christian Sources for Social Change* (New York: Paulist Press, 1977), p. 69. Emphasis his.

46. Lisa S. Cahill, 'Respecting life and causing death in the medical context', *Concilium* 179 (1985), p. 37.

4

The Ethics
of Punishment

Our fourth area of investigation concerns a sphere of ethics in which few pretensions regarding a healthy tradition are possible. Indeed, when we turn to the subject of punishment we find nothing that even remotely resembles a well-developed tradition. Moreover, anyone who makes a serious study of the history of crime and punishment is likely to be left wondering which of those two activities has caused the greater amount of damage since humans began dwelling on this planet. One learns that, not so very long ago, in countries where such penalties are illegal today, people suffered terrible mutilations, appalling humiliation, banishment and even death for crimes which we might consider to be little more than petty. In spite of this far from inspiring history, punishment – sometimes light, sometimes severe – is still meted out in the so-called advanced civilizations of the Western world as an almost automatic response to crime. What exactly is involved in this process? Why are we doing it? Ought we to be doing it? If not, what should we be doing?

When attempting to answer difficult questions, many of us tend to look to the writings of our wisest forebears. One of those most often consulted is St Thomas Aquinas, who mentions both remedial and deterrent aspects of punishments. Few of us, however, would be totally happy with everything he has to say on the subject. He tells us, for instance, that vengeance is lawful to the extent that the purpose of it is the checking of evil. Some people, he notes, have no virtue, and are dissuaded from sin only through the fear of losing things that are dearer to them than what they would gain by sinning. Reprisal for sin, therefore, should consist in depriving people of the things that are dearest to them. Among these are life, bodily health, personal freedom, wealth, homeland and reputation. The punishment, he goes on to say, should terrify more than the sin attracts.[1] Elsewhere he says that when the civil authority inflicts punishments to deter crime it functions as the instrument of God.[2] Such punishments, it seems, might be quite horrific, although Aquinas discusses them in a matter-of-fact way. In principle, he writes, a healthy, well-functioning limb cannot be removed without doing harm to the whole body of which it is a part. However, the whole man is himself part of a whole community. Suppose, then, that the limb is removed as a penalty to restrain him from sinning. Although his body will still suffer a loss, the community as a whole will benefit. Therefore, he continues, just as a public authority may execute a man for certain major faults, it may remove one of his limbs for a lesser fault.[3] He goes on to add that, provided it is a penalty due in justice, one who has authority over another may resort to beating that person. Thus, by way of chastisement and discipline, a father may legitimately beat his son and a master may legitimately beat his slave.[4] We would not, of course, expect any Christian leader or teacher to repeat all of this today. The ethics of punishment is one of those spheres, of which we have seen several in this book, in which a constant and unchanging Christian tradition is non-existent. Unfortunately, in the case of punishment, what most of us have received by way of what some would call 'tradition', but which might also be referred to simply as inheritance, is, to say the least, somewhat muddled. What, then, are we to make of it?

On the face of it, inflicting punishment would seem to be one of the clearest and most common instances of doing something which is decidedly unpleasant in order that something good might come of it. Of course, common sense, experience and our own moral sensitivities combine to tell us that sometimes it is morally right to cause serious discomfort, irritation, frustration and even to indulge in pain-provoking activity in order to achieve something good. Among other oft-quoted instances, we find: various kinds of surgery, the use of violence in self-defence or in defence of a third party, taking what belongs to another without permission in cases of dire necessity, just war, and telling an untruth to save somebody's life. It might be useful to add in parenthesis at this point that there need not be any clash here with St Paul's teaching that one should not do evil in order that good may come of it (Rom 3:8). Paul was surely saying that one should not do what is morally wrong in order that good may come of it. However, although the general principle may be accepted, the specific question remains: can *punishment* be justified? Where punishment of convicted criminals is concerned, it would seem that most of us are convinced that we do not have sufficient reason for inflicting certain penalties which were often employed by our ancestors. In fact, we are inclined to brand those punishments as inhuman. On the other hand, penalties such as fining and imprisonment, being regarded as less barbaric, have achieved, in the eyes of many people and for quite a long time, an air of respectability – a strangely used word to which we shall return later. Recently, however, the morality of using even those methods of punishment has been the subject of heated debate on both sides of the Atlantic and in other parts of the world. Some people even express doubts about the moral rightness of *any* kind of punishment of criminals. Others merely raise questions about proportion between a crime and its punishment. On that particular point, perhaps we should point out that, in order to have sensible discussion on the subject of proportion in punishment, we need to have some clear idea about the kind of evil(s) involved and, of course, we need to know what we are trying to achieve. Recently, however, it has become increasingly clear that there is no general agreement among us regarding what we are or, indeed, should be trying to achieve. At the same time we have become increasingly aware of the fact that the evil involved in some contemporary punishments, notably imprisonment, can be very great indeed.

WHY DO WE PUNISH?

Punishment shows its face early in most people's lives. For many of us, though certainly not for all, the penalties inflicted by parents and teachers were very mild. Some fundamentalist readers of the Old Testament, however, might look askance at such leniency. After all, the book of Proverbs has clear advice about the salutariness of a good beating. People who fail to use the stick, we are told, hate their children (Prov 13:24). By giving them a stroke of the cane, one saves their souls from Sheol. Besides, it is not likely to be fatal! (Prov 23:13–14). Ben Sirach is even more enthusiastic, claiming that anyone who loves his son will beat him frequently. If you pamper the little beast, we are told, he will terrorize you. So:

> While he is young, do not allow him his freedom and do not wink at his mistakes. Bend his neck in youth, bruise his ribs while he is a child, or else he will grow stubborn and disobedient, and hurt you very deeply. Be strict with your son, and persevere with him, or you will rue his insolence. (Sir 30:11–13)

If this is not enough, the solution is found in Deuteronomy. If a stubborn and rebellious son refuses to pay attention to his parents even when they punish him, his father and mother should take him to the elders at the gate of their town and tell them that their son is a stubborn, rebellious wastrel and drunkard. All his fellow citizens should then stone him to death. 'You must banish this evil from among you. All Israel, hearing of this, will be afraid' (Deut 21:18–21). One imagines that, even in ancient Israel, not many people took this last-mentioned piece of advice literally. There is evidence to suggest, however, that, in certain later periods, it became fashionable, at least among certain classes, to treat children severely. One such period, as far as certain parts of the Western world are concerned, would seem to be the latter half of the nineteenth century. Terence P. Morris notes that the puritanical authoritarianism that was characteristic of upper- and middle-class families was mirrored throughout society in Victorian England and, to some extent, among the well-to-do in the United States and Continental Europe. It was only with the publication of the early work of Sigmund Freud, he believes, that doubt began seriously to be expressed about such reliance upon repression and physical punishment in the rearing of children:

> Perhaps the most important conclusion to be drawn from Freud's work in this context is that punishment, particularly work [*sic*] of a physical nature, is often related at an unconscious level with disturbances and anxieties within the punisher. Through the mechanism of projection the parent may thus punish what he feels guilty about himself; a parent who is himself sexually repressed may, for example, punish a child for looking at representations of the female body or for masturbation. Punishment may also be inspired by the sadistic sexual tendencies of the parent. Equally, it is now generally accepted among experts in the field of child care that physical punishments, especially when applied in the anal region, may result in erotic stimulation of an unhealthy nature.[5]

Certain forms of child punishment which, it seems, were regarded as normal a century ago would now come under the heading of child abuse. Perhaps Victorian parents thought they found justification for their actions in the passages from the Old Testament referred to above, but, if that is so, St Paul's advice to parents not to drive their children to resentment (Eph 6:4) presumably went unnoticed by them or was treated to a special kind of interpretation. Even without taking Paul's words into account, however, there might have been a less enthusiastic rush to punish if more Victorians had stopped to reflect upon the fact that in the books of the Old Testament we find the story of a people's struggle to grow. The Israelites learned only very slowly how to apply even some of their own most basic teachings to particular spheres of human morality. It is worth pointing out that the failure to notice this on the part of some people during the eighteenth and nineteenth centuries resulted not only in the discovery of biblically based arguments in favour of harsh punishment, but also in biblically based arguments which supported the institution of slavery.

In most Western countries there would seem to have been something of a softening in the general approach to the punishment of children during the twentieth century. In recent years, however, there has also been a good deal of discussion about the danger of letting children go unchecked, of being too permissive. Experience, we are told, indicates that punishment of children in moderation is sometimes advisable. Nevertheless, serious reservations have been expressed about the advisability of smacking. Indeed, legislation has been introduced in some countries to make the practice illegal – even for parents. Moreover, 'An investigation carried out for Epoch (End Physical Punishment of Children), which monitored 700 families for 30 years, established a link between smacking children when young and delinquency in teenagers'.[6]

An important thing to note in debates about child punishment is that, although enormous mistakes have been made over the years, and although there may sometimes have been ulterior motives of which the punishers themselves were not always clearly aware, there would now appear to be a good deal of agreement, at least among scholars investigating such matters, regarding the normal, legitimate reason for such punishment. For most, it seems, it is part of a training process, an educational tool, one of the ways in which parents and others try to help the child to become a better person. A problem of no mean proportions arises, however, when we try to apply the same sort of reasoning to quite different contexts. It is tempting to draw a parallel, for instance, between this disciplining of children and punishment inflicted upon criminals – indeed people often do. But is such drawing of parallels helpful? After all, children – ideally at least – are chastised by people who love, care for and protect them. In cases in which their parents or guardians do not love them, there must be serious doubt about the salutariness of any punishment. What, then, are we to make of the punishment of criminals? Do the people who punish them also love them? There are, I would venture to suggest, some grounds for doubt here, a doubt to be applied to the vast majority of cases.

Now some may claim that our aim in sending people to prison, for instance, is their betterment or reformation, and the wide use of the word 'correction', especially in the law-enforcement system of the United States, might lead to a strengthening of that view. However, a glance at the available literature on crime and punishment and an awareness of common attitudes in society lead to a very different conclusion. At this point, suffice it to mention the fact that prisons in many of the rich democracies are seriously overcrowded, that sanitary conditions in a noticeable percentage are appalling, and that such conditions do not seem to figure as truly major points for discussion (if they are mentioned at all) during election campaigns in most of those same democracies.

Why, then, do we punish criminals? That, it seems to me, is not the easiest of questions to answer. Fortunately, however, we do not have to start from scratch. A number of scholars have attempted an investigation into how state punishment of criminals came to be, while others have attempted to justify the existence of the practice. A glance at their writings will perhaps shed a little light on things.

THE PUNISHMENT OF CRIMINALS

Leo Page supposes that the earliest offences were crimes of violence. In primitive times, he says, personal revenge was the natural and obvious remedy for them. Theft became a prominent offence as the notion of private ownership developed:

> In such cases it was seen that the first essential of justice was the restitution of the stolen property; where this was not possible, similar stock or goods belonging to the thief could be taken; soon there must have arisen the idea of taking from him goods of greater value than those stolen, with the double object of his punishment and of compensation to the injured party for the trouble to which he had been put.

Inasmuch as it took the place of private vengeance, Page sees the institution of this system of compensation as an important step in the history of law. At its inception, he says, it was the custom that the elders of the tribe would declare the sum which they considered the offender should pay. The injured party was, however, free to refuse such an offer and to insist upon his right to the blood feud. This was, of course, more likely to happen in cases involving violence and/or loss of life than in those involving only offences against property. As civilization progressed, however, it would seem that, even where violent crime was concerned, people came to see the advantages of arrangements of compensation over what Page calls 'the illogical violence and arbitrary results of fights between surviving relatives'. At first this system was available only where private wrongs were concerned. It could not be applied to public offences which endangered the safety of the community. The ancient remedy for these public offences was expulsion from the tribe, but, as society became more highly organized, this penalty was seen to be unsatisfactory. People who had thus been driven into the forest were allowed to return if they would submit to a punishment.

In order to keep supremacy, notes Page, a king or chief needed ordered peace and quiet. Crimes of public disorder and violence were therefore repressed with severity as crimes against the sovereign and the state. Such crimes 'against the King's Peace' were regarded as different in degree and kind from private wrongs between individual subjects. Eventually, however, some of these latter also came to be gathered into the concept of crimes against the King's Peace:

> As the power of the king grew, an ever increasing number of offences were brought into the same category. In this progressive extension of the ambit of the King's Peace we may trace the growth of the public (or what is called today the criminal) as distinct from the private (or what is called today the civil) law.[7]

With slight variations here and there,[8] Page's description of how the punishment of criminals came to be the responsibility of the state would seem to coincide with those of other scholars. As regards the *right* of the state to punish, large numbers, I imagine, would agree with Richard Swinburne's claim that it sometimes derives from its being the victim and sometimes from its ability to act on behalf of the victim.[9] It would not be clear to everybody, however, that a right to punish necessarily results from the mere fact that the state is a victim or takes the part of the victim. Moreover, having said all of this, we still need to ask about the very *raison d'être* of the punishment of criminals, whether inflicted by the state or by a private individual.

THE MEANING OF PUNISHMENT AND ITS JUSTIFICATION

A commonly suggested justification for punishment is deterrence. Patrick Pringle found a clear exposition of this theory in words addressed by the eighteenth-century English judge Sir Thomas Burnet to a man whom he had just sentenced to death. ' "It is very hard, my Lord," said the convicted felon, "to hang a poor man for stealing a horse." "You are not to be hanged for stealing a horse," Sir Thomas replied, "but you are to be hanged that horses may not be stolen." ' [10] If one looks at things from a purely consequentialist point of view, however, the question that immediately comes to mind regarding this matter is whether or not particular penalties will succeed in deterring people from particular criminal activities.

Much, of course, depends upon the circumstances. If, for instance, people in a certain place are stealing food out of dire necessity, it is doubtful that the threat of long prison sentences will have much effect. Obviously, the dire necessity involved in this case adds ethical complications of its own, but my purpose in citing it here is merely to show how the effectiveness of a punishment as a deterrent is likely to vary in different contexts. Even in a more general sense, the usefulness of *capital* punishment as a means of deterring people from certain crimes is certainly to be doubted. In a book published in 1989, Ruth Morris reported that, since the abolition of capital punishment in Canada, the homicide rate had dropped from 3.09 per 100,000 to 2.74. She also noted that no consistent differences were seen when comparisons were made between states in the USA which had capital punishment and neighbouring states that did not. She adds: 'My own favourite story on deterrence is that the reason they had to discontinue the public hangings of pickpockets in 17th century England was not humanity: there were too many pickpockets operating in the crowds watching the public hangings.' [11]

To make matters worse, there are some indications that certain forms of punishment intended to have a deterrent effect have sometimes actually played a part in encouraging or promoting crime. Is it not likely, for instance, that public floggings, mutilations and executions, far from discouraging violence in society, positively promoted it? Commenting on the gradual movement away from punishment as a public spectacle in some Western countries, Michel Foucault noted that:

> whatever theatrical elements it [punishment] still retained were now downgraded, as if the functions of the penal ceremony were gradually ceasing to be understood, as if this rite that 'concluded the crime' was suspected of being in some undesirable way linked with it. It was as if the punishment was thought to equal, if not to exceed, in savagery the crime itself, to accustom the spectators to a ferocity from which one wished to divert them, to show them the frequency of crime, to make the executioner resemble a criminal, judges murderers, to reverse roles at the last moment, to make the tortured criminal an object of pity or admiration. As early as 1764, Beccaria remarked: 'The murder that is depicted as a horrible crime is repeated in cold blood, remorselessly' . . . The public execution is now seen as a hearth in which violence bursts again into flame.[12]

It is not only when punishment becomes a public spectacle, however, that it can have a corrupting influence. At least as long ago as the latter half of the seventeenth century it was claimed that people became debauched in prison in England and came out instructed in the arts of thievery and lewdness.[13] Although insufficient research has been carried out in this area, and notwithstanding the fact that many people are quite obviously not corrupted in prison, there are certainly grounds for concern that, even today, some people are. Concern has also been expressed about the possible counter-productivity of forms of punishment which involve loss of prestige, such as, for instance, the publication of criminal proceedings in newspapers. More than forty years ago Sir Norwood East noted that such a policy can be double-edged if publicity satisfies the vanity of the offender or that of his or her relations:

> In a recent case of murder, with which I was concerned, the mother of the homicide was reported to be mentally defective or very backward. She was delighted when told that her son had been arrested for murder, and said that 'she never thought he would be clever enough to get his name in the papers'. Curtis H. Clay, Managing Editor, *Daily Post Tribune*, La Salle, Illinois, has stated: 'Since crime was banned from our page one, offences committed by local residents have been few and of a minor nature.' In 1909, Judge H. T. Hulbert, Head of the Wayne County, Detroit, Juvenile Court, persuaded the editors of four papers to cut out entirely, or tone down, the notices of crimes in which juveniles figured. J. N. Baker reports that delinquency was reduced so much that 'the court practically went out of business'.[14]

Such factors raise doubts concerning the morality of using certain kinds of punishments as deterrents in certain situations. Nevertheless, in spite of all that we have said so far, we must face the possibility – perhaps we should say probability – that some people are deterred from crime when they see what happens to others whose crimes have been discovered. There is, however, a reason for rejecting deterrence as a justification for punishment which is far weightier than any we have considered thus far. To cause suffering to somebody merely in order to strike so much terror into others that they will thereby be deterred from acting in a particular way is surely abuse of a human person. Such deterrence may well be an additional bonus, so to speak, if the person punished is justifiably so punished, but the fact remains that we still need to find a justification for punishing that person in the first place.

In spite of what we noted earlier about the corruption and deterioration that may often result from punishment, there are still those who claim that, in theory at least, the *raison d'être* and the justification of punishment are to be found in the reformation and rehabilitation of the criminal. The thinking of people who speak thus would seem to be that punishment can bring a person to his or her senses, that it can be just as much an educational tool for adults as it is for naughty children. More than a few of them would, of course, go on to say that something more than punishment is needed for a complete conversion process, but that punishment is a valid part of that process. Many critics would, no doubt, argue that, although something like this may happen at least some of the time when children are punished, there must be serious doubts about the validity of such a theory when applied in an unloving atmosphere to adult criminals. Certainly, there would seem to be no grounds for justification of those prison systems of the not too distant past which imposed silence, solitude and attendance at Christian prayer services on inmates. If the counter-productivity of such schemes was not obvious at the time to those responsible for their implementation, hindsight has since provided us with the necessary 20/20 vision. Nevertheless, we should surely be prepared to make resources available which would assist reformation and rehabilitation where they are required and requested. In recent times more than one sex offender who has committed a similar offence again after release from prison has spoken of an unfulfilled wish to receive therapy in prison. If such resources were made available, however, we should note that the reformation and rehabilitation would not be punishment, although the therapy might accompany the punishment. In other words, the punishment would require another justification.

The word 'retribution' is an important one in discussions about punishment, but it is certainly not the easiest to grasp hold of and to explain. Dictionaries do not help because they tend to include revenge as one of its meanings, and that is a meaning which many, perhaps most, of those who write in favour of retributivist theories of punishment strive to disown. They tend to see retribution in the realm of justice. Although we are far from anything resembling agreement on a thoroughly satisfactory theory of justice, there is at least a fairly general acceptance that justice is about giving each person his or her due. In this context, retribution is what is due to the wrongdoer. It is what he or she deserves. It serves him or her right.

Such notions are clearly contained in the following words of Pius XII, although the Pope was evidently also concerned with the reformation of the criminal:

> The punishment is the reaction, required by law and justice, to the crime: they are like a blow and a counter-blow. The order violated by the criminal act demands the restoration and re-establishment of the equilibrium which has been disturbed. It is the proper task of law and justice to guard and preserve the harmony between duty, on the one hand, and the law, on the other, and to re-establish this harmony, if it has been injured. The punishment in itself touches not the criminal act, but the author of it, his person, his Ego, which, with conscious determination, has performed the criminal act . . .
>
> Punishment properly so-called cannot therefore have any other meaning and purpose than that just mentioned: to bring back again into the order of duty the violator of the law, who had withdrawn from it. This order of duty is necessarily an expression of the order of being, of the order of the true and the good, which alone has the right of existence, in opposition to error and evil, which stand for that which should not exist.[15]

Most theories of punishment, be they based on retribution, rehabilitation or deterrence, remain unconvincing, not least because they lack development and do not deal sufficiently well with the problem that punishment so often simply makes matters worse. Some years ago, however, the Anglican scholar Sir Walter Moberly did succeed in developing a theory of some substance. He also faced the problems head on. No doubt, not all his readers have been convinced by his arguments, but the theory is a fascinating one based on valuable insights about human behaviour. Fascinating though it may be, however, Moberly's theory, it seems to me, is not sufficiently well known to be considered part of the generally received wisdom of most Christians, even in the West. Let me, therefore, briefly describe it. 'It is true', he says, 'that the real battle between good and evil in the human soul takes place in a region deeper than any which punishment can reach directly. Yet, a punishment may be intended to reflect this battle, and, indirectly, to influence its course; and such an aim need not be merely delusive.'

He sees punishment as a form of ritual which represents the moral deterioration which is taking place in the wrongdoer. The method employed in punishment is therefore that of forming a kind of picture of this moral deterioration. The only legitimate ground we can have for such portrayal, he says, is our hope that such a display 'may avert consummation of the real thing'. When we punish wrongdoers we seek thereby to make them and others aware of our own 'vivid apprehension of the disastrous import' of their wrongful acts and of the moral danger in which those wrongdoers stand. The punishment serves as a kind of mirror which, so to speak, is held up before the eyes of offenders in order that they may see themselves as they really are. 'The physical pain or material loss inflicted is designed to be a garish but arresting picture of the spiritual injury which he has inflicted both on himself and on his fellows.'

Punishment, Moberly goes on to say, is an alternative to the often gradual and imperceptible process of dying which is the wages of sin. As such, its function resembles that of physical pain as a danger signal. It may open the eyes of the person punished to moral danger. Punishment, he says, is a kind of inverted sacrament inasmuch as its object is not to effect or ratify what it images, but rather to bring it to naught. Further on, Moberly talks about the limitations of punishment. He sees it as being appropriate only in what he refers to as an intermediate moral region. At one end of the scale we find that there are offenders who are too degraded to be capable of undergoing punishment as punishment, and authorities which are too amoral to be capable of imposing it. Punishment (in Moberly's understanding of it as a kind of inverse sacrament) is only possible if the culprit feels that it is deserved. If a person is known or presumed to be incorrigible, to have not even a vestige of moral health, it may be possible to repress or to outlaw, but, strictly speaking, it is not possible to punish (again using that word in the sense described above). Moberly then helpfully quotes his grandfather, who was a mid-nineteenth-century head-master: 'I should never venture to flog a boy who I feared was hopeless or nearly so, but rather send him away. If he be dying of the moral disease, punishment will only make him die sooner and more surely.' If we now look at the other end of the scale, we see more clearly why Moberly refers to an intermediate moral region. It is possible that punishment may be outgrown. 'There may be penitents too whole-hearted to require it for their re-education, communities too advanced morally to need it as an example, tribunals at once so awe-inspiring and so resourcefully creative as to be able to follow the "more excellent way" of St Paul.'

Moberly does not limit the role of punishment to one of education or enlightenment of the offender. Society, he says, cannot remain indifferent to the evil-doing of one of its members. It must do something to rid itself of this centre of infection. He sees some sort of counter-activity as obligatory in order to stop the spread of the infection, to put matters right. Suppose we were to say that sequestration of property, the curtailment of liberty or comfort, or the deprivation of rank or office is, in a particular case, just. We might alternatively say that the punishment fits the crime or that it serves the culprit right. When our meaning is fully analysed, says Moberly, it can be seen that we are saying that the punishment should be designed to symbolize, and be felt to symbolize, the twofold retribution that is inherent in the situation. That twofold retribution is, of course, 'the moral deterioration which is automatic, and the counter stroke which is obligatory'. Such punishment, he goes on to say, is retributive in the sense that, in a symbolic, though very rough, way, it depicts the true retribution of what the offender has done. The strength of the word 'symbolic' in Moberly's scheme of things needs to be emphasized. If no likeness is recognizable, he says, the punishment can hardly be just. He then goes a little further regarding the matter of 'fitting' a particular crime. He cites some people's suggestions (not all convincing ones to my way of thinking) of punishments that might fit certain crimes. One of these – his own, it would seem – is that imprisonment and excommunication indicate temporary incapacity for membership of society. Pecuniary fines, however, are felt to be an unsatisfactory penalty, he says, because the correspondence between the punishment and the crime is blatantly artificial.[16] Regarding this last point, we might add that most fining of very rich people probably has a similar effect to that of confiscating a single pea from the plate of one earning an average income. It might be suggested that such a gesture is all that is required in some cases because of the pettiness of the offence. However, it is clear that a quite different message is likely to be conveyed to a very poor person on whom the same fine is imposed for the same petty offence.

It might be objected that Moberly's way of looking at things goes too far in that it implies some sort of judgement of persons as well as acts. It could also be objected that, even if we accept that society is obliged to do something about the 'infection' resulting from wrongdoing, it does not follow that this 'something' should be punishment. Some medicine is pleasant to taste and has no nasty side effects. At the same time it must be said that there is a case for making people aware, in some way or other, of the fact that certain activities which they perform are likely to have a bad effect upon them. Take, for example the case of a young man who has recently taken up the profession of mugging defenceless people. We may be fairly certain, I imagine, that such activity will not merely hurt his victims, but will also have a devastating effect upon the young man himself. However, we still have to confront an objection similar to the one that was raised about society's obligation to rid itself of the 'infection'. It is not clear why we should use *punishment* to make him aware. After all, there are cases in which a hug would be more effective than a slap across the face or a night in jail. While accepting the validity of this last point, however, we would do well to note that the experience of humankind in general with regard to the correction of children would seem to indicate that there are grounds for resorting to minimum punishments on certain occasions. We might add that there are also grounds for believing that even hugs are likely to be counter-productive in certain situations. We are thus left with the possibility (perhaps most would say 'probability' or even 'certainty') that punishment should sometimes be used to clear away 'infection' and to bring wrongdoers to their senses.

Having said all this, however, we ought not to lose sight of Moberly's use of the expression 'intermediate moral region'. Children, we have noted, are ideally punished by people who love them, care for them and protect them, and, of course, such punishment should never be excessive. We have also noted that if children are punished in anything less than an atmosphere of love of which they are aware, it is doubtful that the punishment will have a thoroughly salutary effect. Add to this Moberly's observation that at one end of the spectrum (below the intermediate moral range) we find authorities which are too amoral to be capable of imposing punishment. We could surely say that many such authorities would be more than capable of making people suffer for the crimes they have committed, and may well be in the habit of doing so. Their making people suffer, however, would not be punishment in the sense which Moberly has given to that word. It might, moreover, be just as damaging as penalties inflicted on offspring by parents who do not love their children, perhaps even more so. Another question, then, springs to mind: which, if any, authorities in this world of ours are capable of administering punishment in Moberly's sense of the word?

WHAT HAPPENS IN PRACTICE?

There are indeed grounds for believing that the punishment of criminals, as it exists today in most countries of the world, does not in any way resemble what Moberly had in mind when he advanced his theory. George Ives's description of it as 'a survival from savagery' would seem to be much nearer the mark. There are also grounds for accepting Ives's assertion that punishment originally grew out of an instinct for retaliation and is instinctively retained for the sake of vengeance. He goes on to say:

> But punishment, besides its antiquity and universality, shows further and stronger traces of its instinctive origin in that we find it resorted to and applied in ways and circumstances which serve no rational or objective purpose; in ways that could not, I should imagine, be defended as rational, by even the thickest-headed advocates of deterrence; in ways so manifestly childish and animistic [*sic*] that, I submit, we cannot account for them except as acts instinctive and concessory.[17]

It is certainly difficult to defend the record of some of the so-called advanced countries of the world against these charges made by Ives. Adrian Speller writes that in 1983 about 400 men and 120 women were imprisoned in Britain for failing to pay a fine imposed for using a television set without having paid the licence fee which is the basic source of funding for the BBC. Speller also reported that, at the time of writing, about 23 per cent of all people received into prison under sentence in Britain were fine defaulters.[18] The widespread use of fining as a penal sanction has often been criticized because of the obvious unfairness built into the system. Even if we were to disregard that matter, however, we would have to say that, in many, perhaps all, cases, the use of imprisonment as a back-up to fines would seem to be an expression of gross irresponsibility. Imprisonment is often a terrible punishment out of all proportion to many of the crimes for which fines are imposed. Indeed, it would seem to be out of all proportion to many of the crimes for which imprisonment is imposed.

One factor which contributes to the horror of imprisonment is the overcrowding that results precisely from sending too many people to prison. Another is the lack of basic facilities, which an authority capable of administering punishment in the sense described by Moberly would surely provide as a matter of course. Again writing about the situation in Britain, Speller writes:

> For thousands of prisoners, the chamberpot in the corner of the cell is the usual toilet facility. Little wonder that prisoners wrap their excrement in newspaper and throw it out of the cell window rather than try to sleep with the smell. Each morning over 26,000 prisoners perform the ritual of slopping out the chamberpots. One prison governor, in evidence to the House of Commons Expenditure Committee in 1978, described how the slopping-out procedure had to be done 'in a cyclical order, in order to provide that the drainage system is not overtaken by events. In other words, it cannot deal with the accumulated effluents collected during the night period.'

Another prison governor has described life in an over-crowded cell as 'like living in a bathroom for seventeen hours a day with two strangers'.[19]

In recent years, this problem has been openly discussed in the British parliament, and a process of improvement has at last begun. However, the problem of the lack of toilet facilities is so great that it will probably take a very long time to resolve. Moreover, there are few signs of the dawning of a real revolution in attitude in Britain or in most other countries.

The authorities concerned may not be capable of administering punishment as Moberly would see it, but they are certainly capable of making offenders suffer. In prison, moreover, offenders may also suffer in ways not intended by the authorities. Such lack of intention does not suffice for a complete exoneration of those same authorities because the sufferings concerned are often a foreseeable offshoot of the prison system as it exists in many countries. In some prisons, for example, the amount of violence, both physical and psychological and sometimes of a sexual nature, which is inflicted on prisoners by fellow inmates is alarming. In 1991, for instance, there was a newspaper report of an incident in a correctional institution in the USA. A young man who had been sentenced to one year for possession of marijuana was sent to a psychological evaluation unit. After two hours the only words he had written on his exam paper were 'Help me. Help me.' It transpired that he had been put into a cell block containing four beds and eleven other inmates. They had sexually assaulted him every hour for 48 hours.[20] It would, of course, be easy to add much more to the list of evils involved in the particular penalty of imprisonment. Such a litany is not necessary for our purposes here, but one item that I feel we should not omit is the immense harm done to families. In spite of all this, however, it would seem that sending people to prison in the United States bears some resemblance to a knee-jerk reaction. In this great democracy, the total population of prisons and jails was reported in 1991 to be in excess of one million.

In most Western countries there are some positive signs. Pressure for the reform of penal systems has resulted in a number of interesting developments which would seem to indicate some movement in the right direction. The development of probation services and the introduction of community service penalties in some countries, for instance, would seem to be something of an improvement on automatic imprisonment. Having said that, however, we should not ignore the all too evident problems of understaffing and underfunding which often seem to dog such projects. Nor should we ignore the effects of the 'get tough on crime' approach of numerous politicians in certain countries. Such a stance on the part of some politicians in the United States is cited by some commentators as one of the main reasons for the alarming growth in the prison population of that country in recent years and for the frenetic rush to build more prisons (at enormous expense) which accompanies that growth. There are indications that there is, in general, a more responsible approach to punishment in some countries than is the case in either the United States or the United Kingdom at the present time. Perhaps, then, there are reasons for being optimistic. Nevertheless, the fact remains that in numerous 'advanced civilizations' offenders are made to suffer for their crimes in ways that can hardly be expected to produce positive results.

Furthermore, we must take into account the effect that all this inflicting of suffering has upon people other than those who are being punished. In the late eighteenth and early nineteenth centuries it would seem that there was much reliance in England upon the deterrent effect of a somewhat barbaric approach to punishment. At the same time, there was, we are told, at least one positive note to record: there were various safeguards against wrongful arrest, unfair trial and false conviction. Unfortunately, however, as Pringle informs us, 'It was precisely because the criminal procedure was so liberal that the laws were so severe. They were not harsh because the people who made them were brutal; it is more likely', and this is the rub, 'that the harshness of the laws helped to brutalize the people.'[21] Most of the overt sadism of earlier times has disappeared from our penal systems, but we would do well to meditate upon the possibly brutalizing or otherwise corrupting effect on the general populace of present-day punishments, such as burying people in prisons where most of us do not witness the suffering they are forced to endure.

WHAT HAS TO BE DONE?

This question may seem out of place here. The reader could feel that, having established that we have inherited little of value on this subject from our forebears and that we continue to make a mess of things, I should simply bring this chapter to an end here. The job I set out to do is done. It seems to me, however, that, in ending thus, I would leave too many loose ends, too many questions unanswered. One obvious such question is: what should we do with criminals? Not to attempt at least the beginnings of an answer would seem to me to be most unsatisfactory.

If we hold that it would be morally wrong to continue with the policies regarding punishment which prevail at present in most Western countries, and if we are also of the opinion that the authorities in those same countries are, for the most part, incapable of administering punishment in any sort of salutary way, what can we suggest for the protection of ordinary citizens in those countries? After all, surely the vast majority of us would agree that one of the principal justifications for the very existence of criminal law is the protection of people from harm. Something quite obviously has to be done to curtail the activities of those who resort to violent crime. That said, however, it must be added that it is also obvious that the present treatment of even violent offenders in many countries should not be allowed to continue. All too often, it would seem, our attitude towards such people could be summed up in the following words: 'If they behave like the wildest of animals, we shall treat them accordingly.' Even if we accept that it is true that such people behave like savage beasts, it is not at all clear how we can seriously hope to stand any chance of bringing them into the human race – if that is the way we view the matter – by treating them in ways which would not even be suited to most non-human animals. Clearly, many authorities will simply have to change their ways.

Nevertheless, where protection of the public against violent offenders is concerned, it would seem that drastic measures are called for. There is clearly a strong – indeed, perhaps we should say overwhelming – case for the detention of the violent in secure places, provided, of course, adequate provision is made for uncharacteristic outbursts, certain so-called 'crimes of passion', etc. Such detention, however, need not be inhumane. The call to love one's enemies clearly demands that it should be totally otherwise. In other words, the places of detention need bear little or no resemblance to present-day prisons. They should, for instance, be more spacious, provide for the development and creative use of talents, permit normal human relationships to flourish, and should be run in such a way that those detained are not in any way infantilized. Detainees should not become totally dependent upon their keepers, but should have the opportunity of developing the sense and practice of reponsibility. This may sound fine in theory, but it seems likely that a good deal of research would be needed before anything like this could be brought into reality.

A point worth making, perhaps, at this stage is that, if we are to make any sense of protection of the public as a justification for detention, extremely dangerous people such as serial killers and serial rapists should be detained for as long as those in a position to judge consider them to be a danger to the public. The present widespread policy of exacting something that is all too similar to vengeance but is called a debt of a fixed number of years results too often in very dangerous people being released and allowed to re-offend when the fixed term comes to an end. Having said this, however, we should add that safeguards would have to be introduced so that people who were no longer a danger to the public were not detained for periods longer than necessary.

We should perhaps also add a word here about recent experiments involving meetings between the perpetrators of crimes and their victims – or, when that is not possible or advisable, meetings between the perpetrators and victims of similar crimes committed by somebody else. Some initial results, I am told, indicate positive therapeutic reactions on the side of the victims and genuine remorse on the part of the criminals. It might be suggested that such meetings could themselves be punitive because, during them, the criminal is made to face up to the results of his or her crime. It would not seem advisable, however, for such 'punishments' to be imposed. It would seem unlikely, in many cases at least, that the same positive results would be achieved if the participation of one or both parties were other than voluntary.

At the bottom end of his scale, it will be recalled, Moberly placed not only authorities who are incapable of salutary punishment, but also incorrigible offenders who are incapable of benefiting from punishment. It could be claimed that among the ranks of these (at least apparently) incorrigible offenders will be numbers of those detained for violent crime. It might seem, therefore, that, in such cases, we could not justify detention as punishment because the inmates would not benefit from it. In answer to this possible objection, let me underline the fact that the protection of the public would seem to provide ample justification for detention in such cases, regardless of whether or not the offender is likely to come to his or her senses as a result of that detention. This is in some ways akin to the justification of violence in cases of self-defence or defence of a third party. At the moment of arrest, the similarity would be even greater if it became necessary to use a minimum of force because the person involved offered violent resistance. It is also possible, of course, that very violent people might need to be forcibly restrained on occasions during their detention, although the more humane centres of detention envisaged would be far less likely than present-day prisons to be themselves the initial provocation for violent outbursts.

Having adopted such a minimalizing attitude to violence and segregation, we might be tempted to think that we have said all that is to be said, but that is far from the truth. We have attempted to justify segregation as something other than punishment. On that point, the Quaker writer Kimmett Edgar would seem to agree with us. Its use extends beyond punishment, he says, to social control. He goes on to discuss how segregation is used even within prisons. Disruptive prisoners are separated from the others. As Edgar sees things, this policy can cause serious problems:

> The identification of dangerous prisoners contributes to their difficulties in relating to others. To label anyone dangerous damages that person. The stigma of rejection and abhorrence is incorporated into his self-image. The prisoner must carry the burden of society's fear and rage, directed at him. It is not surprising that such prisoners seem overwhelmed by their own capacity for violence.
>
> We can maintain our faith in segregation as a cure for violence only if we ignore the harm it inflicts on the prison community, and on those we banish. To address prison violence simply by identifying problem prisoners veils the environmental factors that will continue to create problems.[22]

It might be said in reply by some people that resorting to segregation is sometimes forced upon us. We would rather not do it, but we have to. That may be true, but, bearing in mind those words of Edgar, we would do well to reflect on the fact that many of us have a tendency to claim far too easily that certain actions are forced upon us. The truth of the matter is that we can resort even to drastic measures simply out of habit or because it is standard practice in such cases. Moreover, the fact remains that the responsibility of those in authority does not stop at the level of social control through fear and domination. At this point it might be useful to add a word, in parenthesis, so to speak, about the prevention of violent crime, which inevitably also means the prevention of punishment or oppressive social control as a response to violent crime. Because punishment is something nasty done to another person, any attempt to discuss the ethics of the subject must include the prevention of its being needed. It would seem that nothing like enough attention has been given to this subject.

It is easy to understand why some of those in positions of authority feel that they should respond to an increase in violence with a 'get tough on crime' policy. The clearest example of such a policy in the Western world would seem to be that of the United States. Ted R. Gurr notes that there was a very substantial increase in serious crimes against persons there and, indeed, in most European countries during the 1960s and 1970s. Comparisons made between Western Europe and the USA regarding the period 1980–84, however, showed marked differences of magnitude:

> In 1984 the U.S. homicide rate was five times greater than in Western Europe: 7.9 homicides per 100,000 people contrasted with an average rate of 1.5 in European countries. Reported rapes were more than six times as common in the United States (35.7 vs. 5.4 per 100,000 in Europe), robberies four times as common (205 vs. 49 per 100,000).[23]

One of the most obvious results of 'getting tough' in this situation has been the remarkable increase in the prison population in the United States. Between 1950 and 1989 the total number of people behind bars in the land of the free rose from 264,500 to 999,400.[24] As we have already seen, the numbers continued to rise after 1989. All this, it seems, as, I imagine, many would have predicted, has been to no avail.

David Ellis recently reported that, having seen how strict enforcement alone has failed to curb the slaughter, several cities in the United States have introduced programmes aimed at sensitizing children to the effects of violence.[25] Gurr's research would seem to indicate that such a policy is likely to produce a decrease in serious crime statistics. Referring to evidence of a long-term decline in violent crime in some Western countries up to the 1960s, he suggests that a plausible explanation for it could be found in a certain 'civilizing' process which took place in those same countries. It would seem that a cultural process of sensitization to violence first took root among the upper and middle classes in towns, 'and only gradually and selectively was promulgated among rural people and the lower classes'. Among examples of those responsible for the spread of the message he mentions 'churches like the Methodists, who were especially active in British working-class neighborhoods'. In addition to a decline in the homicide and assault rates, this process of civilization also led to what he calls the humanization and rationalization of social policy. 'It led, for example, to the decline and ultimate abandonment of executions in most Western nations, the end of slavery and the brutalization of wage labor, the passing of corporal punishment in schools and prisons, and many other humane features of contemporary life that are often taken for granted.'[26] We could add here that a significant improvement regarding homicide is indicated earlier in his study, where he provides us with some statistics about parts of thirteenth-century England: 'The average annual homicide rates for five rural counties, studied at scattered intervals between 1202 and 1276, ranged from 9 per 100,000 population in Norfolk to 23 in Kent, compared with a contemporary rate of about 2 per

100,000 in all of England and Wales.' Regarding the city of Oxford, he adds that 'Hammer's very thorough study for the 1340s shows an extraordinarily high rate of about 110 homicides per 100,000'.[27] Many people, no doubt, would wish to point to the fact that records like those we keep today are simply not available for the thirteenth and fourteenth centuries. That is quite evidently true, but historical research based on the information that is available does seem to point to a significant improvement in recent times, at least as far as certain parts of the world are concerned. Eric H. Monkkonen also refers to the fact that violent crime occurred very frequently during the Middle Ages, and adds that the rate of such crime has been declining in what is now the industrialized world since then: 'The United States has shared in this decline, but its decline has been much less steep and far more uneven.'[28]

Given the above evidence, there may be some grounds for hoping that the notable increase in violent crime that has taken place in many Western countries during the last couple of decades is merely a temporary deviation from the long-term downward trend. Gurr, however, gives some attention to it, and mentions among likely contributory factors the demographic explosion of young people, the transition to post-industrial society and high unemployment. This last mentioned, he points out, leads to at least some people having ample time and reasons for activity that is both exciting and illegal.[29] In these circumstances, there would seem to be a need to increase efforts to sensitize people – especially the young – to the effects of violence. Perhaps there should even be some revision of the stories regularly told to children about so-called superheroes who regularly solve problems through the use of violence, and seldom seem to use more pacific methods.

Any resulting decrease in violence would inevitably be accompanied by a decrease in punishment. It might be advisable here to alter an old adage and say that it would be like feeding two birds in one hand. Punishment, like war, should be seen as a last resort, and, again like war, as very often an admission of failure on the part of those of us who claim to be on the 'right' side.

NON-VIOLENT OFFENDERS

So much for violent crime, but there are other matters with which we need to deal. As indicated above (p. 132) a very large percentage of offenders who are now serving prison sentences in our Western societies, and, indeed, throughout the world, are not violent people. What are we to do about them? Consider the case of a person who breaks into houses and steals things but does not threaten or injure anybody in the process. Consider too the case of a person who steals people's wallets and purses when he or she sees that they are distracted by something else. Again no physical violence or threatening behaviour is involved. In a very real sense, however, these offences can still be described as crimes against persons. Powerful feelings of personal violation are sometimes experienced in such cases. The victims may feel dirty, abused and alarmingly vulnerable to further evil. Is it not, therefore, important to provide protection against these kinds of criminals too? With the need for protection in mind, we could go on adding to the list of 'candidate' offences, some of which would be much further removed from the 'crimes against the person' category than those which we have just discussed. It could be claimed, for instance, that the theft of large sums of money from financial institutions causes such serious problems of insecurity and perhaps even instability in society that it cannot be tolerated. It would indeed seem that, in all of these cases, and in many others, Moberly is right in claiming that society needs to do something about the infection. Surely it is also right that the offenders should be helped to come to their senses, so to speak, and it may well be that, in many cases, some form of punishment is the best way to do that. Obviously, however, we need to give a good deal more thought than we (by which I mean the whole human race) have given so far to the appropriateness of particular punishments for particular people who have committed particular offences.

CONCLUDING REMARKS

Early in this chapter we looked at the likely origins of punishment by the state instead of by individuals. We also looked briefly at some of the ways in which it is applied in certain countries. In theory there are many advantages to such a system, and that could also be the case in practice if there were a few changes in attitude. Perhaps the most obvious advantage is the fact that the representatives of the state are less likely than the victim to seek revenge or to exaggerate in their response to the crime. There are, however, other advantages. Notwithstanding the Christian call to forgive and to love one's enemies, it does seem to be important, especially after the most violating of crimes, that the victim should be allowed to be angry. Suppressing such a powerful emotion can be damaging. Being aware of it, however, accepting its existence and being able, to some extent at least, to share one's experience of it with others, would seem to be part, perhaps a necessary part, of a healing process. This, it is to be hoped, will culminate in the victim's being able to let go of the whole affair and thus no longer be a victim. This whole process can take place much more easily and more constructively if the responsibility for dealing with the perpetrator of the outrage can be left to the state. The victim should also benefit from the sense of solidarity that arises when he or she knows that the representatives of the state will do whatever is necessary regarding the offender. It would seem to be more than a little unrealistic to expect a victim of gross violation to express love of this particular enemy in ways that amount to truly taking care of the offender. The need for somebody to do so, however, is one of the most important conclusions to be drawn from our discussion of Moberly's insights. The offender is sometimes referred to as a 'public enemy' – most especially, perhaps, in the United States. The Christian call to love such an enemy is, however, always there. If that love can best be expressed in certain situations (at least partially) by certain signs of disapproval or even by a particular kind of punishment, then surely that best expression should be made. If, however, the offender appears to be incapable of benefiting from punishment, the representatives of the state still have the duty of protecting the members of society. It may thus happen, for instance, that detention of that same offender is forced upon them by his or her actions.

In much of what we have said so far we have highlighted the importance of persons and relationships. It is easy to see the need for the expression of love and solidarity towards the victims of crime. Problems arise chiefly when we come to discuss the need to love the perpetrators. St Paul's plea to do everything in love (1 Cor 16:13–14) admits of no exceptions, but, for some people, it undoubtedly seems naïve to attempt to apply that teaching to situations involving serious conflict between persons. Much of the apparent disagreement here, however, would seem to stem from misunderstandings concerning the various shades of meaning of the word 'love'. To use an extreme example, it would be ridiculous to say that a person who finds it necessary to kill an assailant should be fond of that person, be attracted to him or her – romantically or otherwise – while involved in the act of killing. That cannot be what Paul intended. Nevertheless, according to what I see to be his understanding of things, it would be possible to kill the assailant without making an exception to the teaching that everything done should be done in love – or in *agapē* to use his own terminology. In Paul's scheme of things, it would seem that even such an act could and should be done in co-operation with – even under the inspiration of – the Holy Spirit who lives in one's personality. If that is the case with killing in self-defence or in defence of a third party, surely it can be the case with punishment. If it were not so, if punishment by its very nature could never be an act of love, then it could surely never be justified. In this chapter I have remained open to the possibility that it can be, although probably not in the way in which it is usually administered in most societies to the people we call criminals. The accumulated wisdom of humankind concerning this matter, which was passed on to us by our forebears, is simply not good enough. Radical changes in our approach to this subject would seem to be urgently needed.

Another point that strikes me is that we must beware of punishing people for merely being different, although much of what we inherited from our forebears seems to suggest that we should do precisely that. We are constantly in danger of being corrupted by the cancerous growth that we commonly call 'respectability'. That word and its adjective are widely employed to identify people who act in a manner which some anonymous 'they' have decided is acceptable. Those who act differently are apparently not respectable – a dangerous term to use given the fact that its literal meaning is 'worthy of respect'. To take a fairly banal example, not so very long ago (and even today in certain sections of society), hair on men's heads which reached beyond a certain length was regarded by many as a sign of loutishness or else of some other lowly form of life, the Jesus of tradition being, for some unknown reason, exempted from such judgements. Now, those who know about such things inform us that the so-called domestic cat is really still something of a wild animal. It does not submit to human mastery in the way that most dogs do. Usually, no major problem arises out of this for those who wish to have cats as pets because, in general, it would seem that cats, wild though they may be, are quite content to live with humans. Many humans, of course, are equally content to live with cats. Others are not, but that is usually no problem because they do not usually have to live with them. The same is true with regard to incompatible humans. They do not usually have to live under the same roof. Some of us, however, have a tendency to expand our exclusion zones far beyond the boundaries of our own homes. We see people who are not dangerous but of whom we do not approve, who do not live under our roof, but who do walk on the same streets that we walk along. We want them to change their ways. Perhaps we try in various ways to encourage or even force them to change, to become more compatible with us, or, if you like, to become more 'respectable'. In extreme cases, we seek to remove them from our streets or introduce laws against their ways of behaving, just as some people might like to introduce legislation to ban cats from the Colosseum in Rome. Some readers may feel that, apart from the problem of long-haired males, there is little cause for concern about such matters. A little reflection, however, might indicate otherwise. It is probable that, long before the Iron Curtain was torn down, some people in the United States who respected the opinions of others and had no liking for violent revolution saw a value in socialism, even in communism. In the same period, I imagine, some people in the Republic of Ireland bought and sold contraceptives on the black market because they genuinely believed that they were a fine aid to responsible parenthood. One final example: long before the promulgation of laws concerning equality, there were ladies in puritanical parts of Britain and several other countries who wanted to walk into bars unaccompanied by men and buy drinks without being branded as people of loose morals. I believe I have made my point. Respectability usually has a great deal to do with conforming to inherited standards – tradition, if you like – but how often has it anything to do with received wisdom?

Some years ago, in a book entitled *Change: Principles of Problem Formation and Problem Resolution*, Paul Watzlawick, John Weakland and Richard Fisch made reference to attempts to bring about change regarding difficulties which, for all practical purposes, are either non-existent or unchangeable. Much of what has just been said about punishment of those who do not conform to certain patterns, it seems to me, could be put under the heading of attempts to resolve non-existent difficulties. Turning to the subject of attempts to change the unchangeable, we can make use of an example provided by the aforementioned authors:

> Alcoholism is a serious social problem. Restrictions must therefore be placed on the consumption of alcohol, and when this does not eliminate the problem, more of the same is carried to its ultimate – prohibition. But prohibition as the cure of this social evil turns out to be worse than the disease: alcoholism rises, a whole clandestine industry comes into existence, the low quality of its products makes alcohol into even more of a public health problem, a special police force is needed to hunt down the bootleggers and in the process becomes unusually corrupt, etc., etc. As the problem thus worsens, the enforcement of prohibition is made more stringent, but here *more of the same* 'surprisingly' does not produce the desired change. On the contrary, the 'solution' greatly contributes to the problem – in fact, it eventually becomes the greater of the two evils.[30]

If shifting certain previously acceptable activities (like, for instance, the producing and selling of alcoholic beverages) into the category of punishable offences brings in its train such a catalogue of evils as that listed above, clearly, such a move cannot be justified. Often, however, people in positions of authority feel that they must do something about certain social diseases even though it is clear to everybody that, with nothing better than punishment at our disposal, our chances of eliminating those diseases are negligible, while our chances of worsening the situation by means of the 'cure' are very good indeed.[31]

Finally, let us return briefly to the subject of crime prevention, but let us extend it beyond the sphere of violent crime. Acquisitiveness and the conviction that what is mine is exclusively mine seems to be deeply rooted in many contemporary societies. This state of things inevitably gives rise to feelings of greed, anger, envy, and sometimes just plain need in some of those who have very little. There are grounds for thinking that, in many societies, there would be a reduction in the number of crimes such as theft and damage to property, and, of course, a reduction in the amount of punishment meted out to the perpetrators of such crimes (which, indeed, are not always crimes in the wider, non-legal sense of the word) if a more Christian attitude to the ownership of property were taken on board. Here, it seems to me, a selective glance at tradition could be useful. The goods of creation are for all of us, said several of the Fathers of the Church. Those who 'own' things are merely the stewards of those things, and should use them well on behalf of all of us.[32] Unfortunately, however, some stewards have been known to decide that they are exclusive owners of what they possess. They thus offend against their fellow humans, although, in most societies, most of these owners (or stewards gone astray) seem to succeed in remaining on the 'right' side of the law and are thus not likely to be punished for the human tragedies which their proprietorial stance causes.

Here, as in the case of violent crime, it would seem that there is a great need for sensitization. Obviously, if we are to take into account what we have just said, such sensitization should not merely involve what we have come to call 'respect for other people's property'. We should concern ourselves much more simply with respect for other people, notably those who have little or no property. If, however, we in the Christian churches felt tempted to initiate programmes of such sensitization, we would do well to indulge first in an examination of conscience. Although there are some exceptions, it seems to me that, in most of the major Christian bodies in recent times, precious little time and effort have been devoted to the propagation of the so-called 'traditional' teachings of the Fathers regarding private property. There would also seem to be a case for suggesting that some of these bodies, as corporate bodies, and, of course, some of their members as individuals, have become too acquisitive and horrifyingly 'respectable'. Some might suggest that there is here a case for punishment which might bring us to our senses, but maybe a little self-examination and some self-administered penance will do the trick in this case.

NOTES

1. Thomas Aquinas, *Summa theologiae* IIa IIae, q. 108, art. 3.
2. Ibid., IIa IIae, q. 19, art. 3.
3. Ibid., IIa IIae, q. 65, art. 1.
4. Ibid., art. 2.
5. Terence P. Morris, 'Punishment', subsection of 'Crime and punishment' in *The New Encyclopædia Britannica* (Chicago: Encyclopædia Britannica, 1985), vol. 16, pp. 859-60.
6. Sarah Lonsdale, 'Smacking children may be made illegal', *The Observer* (4 May 1992), p. 1.
7. Leo Page, *Crime and the Community* (London: Faber & Faber, 1937), pp. 42-5.
8. See, for instance, Anthony Babington, *The Power to Silence: A History of Punishment in Britain* (London: Robert Maxwell, 1968), pp. 3-5.
9. Richard Swinburne, *Responsibility and Atonement* (Oxford: Clarendon Press, 1989), pp. 99-102.
10. Patrick Pringle, *Hue and Cry: The Birth of the British Police* (London: Museum Press, 1955), p. 48.
11. Ruth Morris, *Crumbling Walls . . . Why Prisons Fail* (London: Mosaic Press, 1989), p. 110.
12. Michel Foucault, *Discipline and Punish: The Birth of the Prison* (London: Penguin Books, 1991), p. 9.
13. Statute of Charles II quoted in George Ives, *A History of Penal Methods: Criminals, Witches, Lunatics* (Montclair, NJ: Patterson Smith, 1970), p. 16.
14. Sir Norwood East, *Society and the Criminal* (London: HMSO, 1949), pp. 191-2.
15. Pius XII, Discourse to the Catholic Jurists of Italy, 5 December 1954. Translation from *Catholic Documents Nos. XI–XX* (London: Salesian Press, 1955), N. XVII, p. 15.
16. Sir Walter Moberly, *The Ethics of Punishment* (London: Faber & Faber, 1968), pp. 199-237.
17. Ives, op. cit., pp. 246-9.
18. Adrian Speller, *Breaking Out: A Christian Critique of Criminal Justice* (London: Hodder & Stoughton, 1986), p. 30.
19. Ibid., pp. 26-7.

20.   See Martin Walker, 'Angry judges hit out at justice by the politicians', *Guardian* (19 June 1991), p. 11.

21.   Pringle, op. cit., pp. 50–1.

22.   Kimmett Edgar, 'Quaker peace and prison violence', *Theology* 95 (1992), p. 105.

23.   Ted R. Gurr, 'Historical trends in violent crime: Europe and the United States' in *Violence in America*, vol. 1: *The History of Crime*, ed. Ted R. Gurr (London: Sage Publications, 1989), p. 21. He notes that there is some debate among experts regarding the accuracy of official data on the magnitude of increases.

24.   Andrew Rutherford, 'Penal reform and prison realities' in *The State of the Prisons – 200 Years On*, ed. Dick Whitfield (London: Routledge, 1991), p. 4.

25.   David Ellis, 'The deadliest year yet' in *Time* (13 January 1992), p. 25.

26.   Gurr, op. cit., pp. 45–6.

27.   Ibid., p. 28.

28.   Eric H. Monkkonen, 'Diverging homicide rates: England and the United States, 1850–1975' in *Violence in America*, ed. Gurr, vol. 1, pp. 80–1.

29.   Gurr, op. cit., p. 48.

30.   Paul Watzlawick, John H. Weakland and Richard Fisch, *Change: Principles of Problem Formation and Problem Resolution* (New York: W. W. Norton & Co., 1974), pp. 31–2.

31.   This is, of course, a very controversial area of debate. Many would assert that prostitution cannot be eliminated and that, when it is made a punishable offence, other problems are added to the original one of prostitution. Accepting this, some would hold that there may still be grounds for exercising some form of control over prostitution without making the mere practice of it illegal. Perhaps even more controversial are calls for the legalization of marijuana. Watzlawick, Weakland and Fisch note that, although nobody can present any evidence for this at present, 'it is a fair guess that the legalization of marijuana (whose ill effects are not certain, but probably not worse than those of many other widely used drugs) might not only decrease its use, but would eliminate almost overnight the complex and counter-productive consequences of its legal suppression, which many experts feel has turned into a cure that is worse than the disease' (op. cit., pp. 88–9). Similar claims are sometimes made regarding pornography.

32.   For an interesting study of this topic, see William J. Walsh and John P. Langan, 'Patristic social consciousness – The Church and the poor' in John C. Haughey (ed.), *The Faith That Does Justice: Examining the Christian Sources for Social Change* (New York: Paulist Press, 1977), pp. 113–51.

5

Building
on the Past

There are in Christian circles certain kinds of situation ethicists who declare that all we need in order to discern moral rightness and moral wrongness is love; that, in any situation, love will tell us what to do. Some of these ethicists might claim that they are traditionalists in the sense that they take their inspiration from the New Testament, from the gospel of *agapē*. The accumulated wisdom which is the fruit of experience, however, appears to have little importance in their scheme of things. Apart from this group, we encounter few moral theologians who do not set great store by that accumulated wisdom. Nevertheless, newcomers to the world of moral theology might well be led by the terminology commonly employed into thinking that this is not the case. In various contemporary debates, for instance, there is a tendency to pin such labels as 'traditionalists' and 'revisionists' on the groups taking part. Like many other labels used in theological and philosophical discourse, these can be very misleading. Far from ignoring or disparaging the wisdom of our forebears, the vast majority of so-called revisionists, it seems to me, attribute great importance to their ethical inheritance. Many might even be happy to call it 'tradition', but they regard this tradition as a dynamic, changing thing. Something similar could perhaps be said about the majority of the so-called 'traditionalists', at least where most matters are concerned, but there are some areas in which they seem to see tradition as more or less static. I say 'more or less static' because, even in some of these areas, some traditionalists admit that quite new problems emerge from time to time and that at least new nuances may be needed to deal with them. We could perhaps say, then, that the differences among the various schools of thought regarding their attitudes to tradition are often differences of degree and little else. However, claims are made about constant and unchanging teachings regarding certain small but important sectors of moral theology, and many traditionalists are quite inflexible in discussion of such matters. These are the areas in which they are most likely to clash with the views of their revisionist colleagues.

In various spheres of knowledge we often refer to a process of development taking place as each generation builds on the discoveries, theories and inventions of its predecessors. Moral theology is no exception. In this regard, Kevin Kelly recently recalled the medieval notion that succeeding generations can see further than their forebears because they are like dwarfs sitting on the shoulders of giants.[1] This is a valuable insight, and one that we would do well to analyse. Quite obviously, it reminds us how important it is continually to bear in mind the accumulated wisdom of those who went before us. It seems to me that we can all too easily fail in this respect and thus find ourselves hanging on to the hem of the giant's coat, thereby seeing even less than our ancestors could see, if we fall into the error of regarding our own age as far superior to any that has gone before and forget where the basis for our presumed superior knowledge is to be found. However, the saying also reminds us that, while it is of immense importance to be aware of our inheritance, it is also important to acknowledge the fact that we too have our own experience and our own capacity to be wise. In other words, to use a different metaphor, we can, and should, build on what previous generations have left us. Only thus will we be able to see from a better vantage point than any they had.

A failure to attribute any importance to our own experience and wisdom amounts to a refusal to accept that such building can take place. It is a failure to accept responsibility. To return to the original metaphor, we can all too easily slip into the role of little children rather than that of truly adult dwarfs. Thus we may fall into the arms of the giant because we are afraid to stand on his shoulders, and, of course, a dwarf in a giant's arms can see no further than the giant can see. It may be that we do not have a good enough reason for changing or developing a particular teaching at a particular time, but it should not be a lack of a sense of responsibility that discourages us from making the necessary investigations.

Already we see that our task is a difficult one, but there is another factor to take into consideration which complicates it even further. Kelly goes on to say that there is a shadow side to tradition, that 'mixed in with the lived experience of wisdom and love in our tradition there is also much unwisdom and unlove'.[2] It was largely because of his keen awareness of this, continues Kelly, that Pope John XXIII felt the need to convoke the Second Vatican Council. In the preceding chapters we have already had reason to note that, on account of sin, misinformation, a lack of insight and probably various other reasons, much of what we have inherited is certainly not wisdom. Thus we find ourselves with the dual task of sorting out the solid foundations from the faulty ones and of continuing the building process. Not easy tasks, but necessary ones.

In recent debate we have seen that, as part of this process of renewal, numerous moral theologians have questioned inherited teachings concerning certain so-called 'absolute' norms of behaviour. These revisionist theologians hold that, although it may be correct to say that such norms apply in the vast majority of cases, it is quite wrong to say that they apply always and everywhere, regardless of circumstances and consequences. It could be said, however, that there is ample evidence to suggest that most of us disagree with our forebears at an even more radical level. We have, seen, for instance, that sexual ethics has had a rather sad and somewhat unhealthy history. Sex, it seems, was regarded by many great teachers in past eras as being in some way evil. We would not expect many moral theologians of our own day, revisionist or traditionalist, to be happy with such a notion. After all, today we stress the importance of accepting one's sexuality and of living happily with one's sexual orientation. Moreover, we often hear psychologists warn us against the dangers of suppression in this sphere. It is also worth noting that we would not expect many moral theologians, revisionist or traditionalist, to agree with much of what was taught in the past regarding the status of each of the sexes and about the possibility of deep friendship and co-operation between people of different genders. Today we stress equality and have at least begun to talk about the need to celebrate our femininity and masculinity. In short, it might be said that there are indications here of fairly major disagreements between generations concerning what it is to be human. Sex and sexuality, moreover, are not the only spheres in which we find scope for such radical disagreement, but, rather than discuss specific areas of special ethics, let us take a look at the centre of things. There we shall see that the differences are very deep-rooted indeed. This exercise, however, will not only highlight the differences between past and present ways of looking at things. It will also help us to see a little more clearly what is involved in the positions of present-day traditionalists and those present-day revisionists who are called proportionalists.

In Germain Grisez's vision of things, human goodness is to be found in the fullness of human being. If, therefore, we wish to understand what is involved in being a good person, we need to ask what are the things that fulfil human persons. These, he says, are the basic human goods, which, important to note, are aspects of persons, and should not, therefore, be thought of as extrinsic.[3] They are: life, health and safety; knowledge and aesthetic experience; some degree of excellence in work and play; living at peace with others, neighbourliness, friendship; peace of conscience and consistency between one's self and its expression; peace with God or the gods, or some non-theistic but more than human source of meaning and value.[4] In contrast to this way of looking at things, Grisez finds St Augustine's theory of the human good suggestive but inadequate. In the latter's scheme of things, he notes, the human person's good is God alone, the good consisting in one's possessing him. This possessing is effected by a mental grasp which produces perfect happiness. The soul which lacks this happiness longs for it restlessly. The good for human persons is therefore essentially peace, or eternal rest. A problem with this theology, continues Grisez, is that it narrows human life down to its religious dimension. The very possibility of a Christian humanism is thus rendered problematical. It could be claimed, of course, that Augustine's concept of peace could be expanded into a more open view, but Grisez points out that there are other human goods which are not simply aspects of peace, according to Augustine's understanding of that term. In this regard, he cites life and health, knowledge of the truth and skill in performance.[5] Further on he accepts that what precisely Augustine had in mind is a question for historians to grapple with, but notes that he has been widely taken up as saying that our life in this world is only a means for reaching heaven and that heaven is an altogether other-worldy goal. Thus the classical position was that the only human fulfilment that should be pursued for its own sake is the enjoyment of God in heaven. This classical view, says Grisez, led to a sharp division between the secular and the religious, the natural and the supernatural, and this division, in turn, tended to undervalue the human goods other than religion. As a result, false conceptions of self-denial and renunciation of the world arose. At their worst, these false conceptions threatened Christian belief in the inherent goodness of creation and in the dignity of human persons as human. Furthermore, religion tended to become totalitarian, this tendency being expressed in the burning of heretics, the suppression of liberty so as to preserve the security of religious institutions, and in the hegemony of clerics.[6]

Grisez, as we have seen, cites knowledge of truth as one of the human goods not included in Augustine's concept of peace. While this may be the case, it would seem, nonetheless, that truth had a special place in the latter's scheme of things. Thus, in his analysis of Augustine's Christian philosophy, we find Etienne Gilson writing:

> Those who claim that they cannot find truth – the sceptic or Academician, for example – cannot possess God or happiness. We know that anyone who does not have what he wants is not happy. Now the sceptic is always in search of truth. He wants to find it; he would like to discover it, but according to his own teaching, this is impossible. Consequently, he can never obtain what he wants. For him, therefore, happiness is impossible. If wisdom, then, implies happiness and happiness implies God, the sceptic can possess neither God, nor happiness, nor wisdom. It is true that Augustine desires truth for the sake of happiness, but he did not think happiness possible apart from truth. The possession of absolute truth is a necessary condition for happiness.

Further on, Gilson adds that, for Augustine, possessing God means possessing wisdom, which, in turn, means grasping God through the mind:

> Our minds can be fully satisfied, our lives called truly happy, only in the perfect knowledge of the Holy Ghost Who leads to Truth, in the enjoyment of Truth itself, and in the union, thanks to Truth, with the Supreme Measure whence it proceeds: Spirit, Truth, Measure; they are but one substance, but one God.[7]

In spite of all this talk about truth, there is nothing here to make us dispute what Grisez says regarding Augustine and the basic goods other than religion, since all of the above is quite obviously part of religion. Already, then, we see major differences between Grisez, who, we have seen, is described by colleagues as a traditionalist, and the great Augustine, but there is more to come.

When he turns to what we might call the secular sphere, and addresses the subject of lying, we see that Augustine always deals with the concept of truth in a special way, even though he does not see it as a basic good in the way that Grisez does. Lying for him means having something in one's heart but saying something else with the intention of deceiving. Having described it thus, he then goes on to teach that one could never be justified in lying, even to save the temporal life of a person. This teaching had enormous influence within the Church for many centuries, and numerous other writers followed Augustine's lead, as John Dedek noted some years ago. In the *Summa Fratris Alexandri*, for instance, he found reference to two reasons for holding that lying could never, under any circumstances, be a morally right act, although the same could not be said of theft and homicide. The first of these reasons is that, where lying is concerned, there is always an evil intention because the person telling the untruth intends to deceive. The second reason is that truth is more noble than either money or life, and no new good could be introduced which could compensate for a defect of truth.[8] Now, regardless of whether or not the writers who held such views had come to see knowledge of truth as one of the basic human goods as described by Grisez, the fact remains that they held truth to be more noble than life. That fact alone makes for major disagreement with those present-day scholars who hold that there is no objective hierarchy among the basic goods. Whatever may have been the thought of scholars of past times regarding the matter, truth, according to Grisez and others of the same school of thought, most certainly is one of the basic human goods. Moreover, looked at from its own point of view, says Grisez, each of those goods is the most important.[9] This is a basic tenet of the school of thought to which he belongs. Some years ago, another member of the school, John Finnis, wrote that 'each of the basic values is equally basic, equally irreducibly and self-evidently attractive'.[10] In short, it seems that Grisez and Finnis would not be inclined to say that truth is more noble than life.

Thus we find quite fundamental disagreements between, on the one hand, Grisez and Finnis (who, we should note again, are generally regarded as being among the more traditional Catholic ethicists), and, on the other, some of the great luminaries of the past (dare we say 'of tradition'?). None of this will be too surprising if we accept that each generation should not just blindly accept the whole of its inheritance; if, in other words, we accept that a certain amount of discernment is called for. Now, Grisez, it would seem, does agree that quite radical changes in teaching about ethics can take place over the years, at least inasmuch as such change or development concerns growth in understanding about the human good. That much is evident in a comment of his on slavery. He notes that the liberty which is violated by slavery pertains to justice. In other words, slavery is an attack upon the basic good of justice and friendship. The aspects of justice involved were less well understood in past times, he writes, but development has since taken place in understanding of the human good, and this has led to a move from condoning slavery to forbidding it: 'The change concerning slavery can be seen as possible because of the unfolding understanding of the human good; now that the development has occurred, we find it hard to see why it did not occur much sooner.'[11]

Many other ethicists of a traditionalist bent would, I am sure, not be alarmed in any way by Grisez's assertions. Indeed, one of the main points I am trying to make here is that traditionalists are not always unwilling to disagree with their forebears, even their most illustrious ones. It is quite evident that they are willing to do so regarding various issues. There are, however, small sectors of ethical teaching regarding which they refuse to acknowledge any justification for breaking with the past. Often among Roman Catholic traditionalists lines are drawn in accordance with current papal opinion and supposed continuity of teaching, although development of sensitivities evidently has a part to play, albeit very slowly in some instances, as is evident in the history of moral teachings concerning slavery. A typical example of Catholic traditionalism is provided by the authors of the so-called 'minority report' of the Pontifical Commission for the Study of Population, Family and Birthrate, who claimed that the Catholic Church could not change its teaching regarding the wrongness of artificial contraception because it could not have erred so atrociously and for such a long time regarding so serious a matter which imposed very heavy burdens on people.[12] Traditionalists are, of course, found in other Christian denominations too. Among their ranks, however, it may be that the absence of the papal factor makes it less difficult to break with supposed continuity of teaching.

What, then, can we say about the revisionist moral theologians? We might simplistically suppose that they are unhampered by the conditioning that comes about in others through the passing on of unwise sayings from past generations, but we would clearly be wrong in so supposing. In practice, revisionist moral theologians are often more traditionalist – even statically so in certain respects – than perhaps even they believe themselves to be. Strangely, at least one factor that can play a major role in preventing members of both schools from embracing the dynamism of tradition is their sense of being up to date, or perhaps I should say, their belief – largely unconscious, I imagine, for it is not usually clearly acknowledged or expressed – that they live in a special age of human enlightenment. Allow me to explain. Numerous moral theologians seem to take it for granted that the list of basic goods to which we have referred is a complete one. Many revisionist theologians as well as traditionalists, it would appear, accept the list in this way, although this is often stated only in an implicit way. This happens in spite of the fact that it is not always easy to see that all the lists that appear in articles and books coincide exactly. The claim, moreover, is a remarkable one, especially when one considers the development that Grisez, and various others, including, of course, revisionists, admit has taken place in this field over the centuries. It seems almost as if a claim is being made that we live in a special era, that humankind – or, at least, moral theologians – have arrived at the end of some sort of investigative journey. Here we see a subtle force at work in the maintenance of static 'tradition'. The makers of the claim, it seems, accept that changes have taken place over the years, but believe that we have now reached a point in which what is left is complete and unchangeable, although it is not at all clear what their basis for such a belief is.

The claim is seen as even more remarkable when one considers that some significant changes occurred only very recently. The history of slavery, to which, as we saw, Grisez refers, provides evidence of that. More such evidence of significant change, within Roman Catholicism at least, is found in the history of religious liberty. We are told that some Catholic theologians even attributed infallibility to the *Syllabus of Errors* which was promulgated by Pius IX in December 1864.[13] Among the 'errors' condemned in this document, however, we find the proposition that it is no longer beneficial that the Catholic Church be considered the only religion of the state to the exclusion of all other forms of worship, and that laws promulgated in some countries which are called Catholic wisely permit strangers going to them to enjoy the public exercise of their own forms of worship.[14] I imagine that most Catholic traditionalists accepted the teaching of the *Syllabus* regarding this matter at least until the publication, after some difficulty, of the *Declaration on Religious Liberty* of the Second Vatican Council.

It could be said, of course, that, in both of these cases, what came about was a growth in awareness of the fact that certain kinds of behaviour constituted attacks on human goods. In other words, the list of such goods has remained the same, but there has been development regarding its implications. On the other hand, it might be countered that, even if we were to accept this as a valid conclusion resulting from an examination of the issues of slavery and religious liberty, there is evidence to suggest that there is disagreement between us and our forebears regarding the matter of human goods at a much more basic level. After all, we have already seen major differences between the positions of Grisez and Augustine. We may therefore be jumping to conclusions too soon about how exhaustive the list is. Even if we disregard that, we should still face up to the possibility that we have simply not come to notice that certain aspects of our behaviour, even today, violate basic human goods, or, indeed, that certain aspects of our behaviour which we now think violate one or more of those goods, do not in fact do so. After all, we saw in an earlier chapter that various changes have taken place over the centuries since the birth of the Church regarding which types of killing are justifiable and which are not. Now, however, it seems that, at least in the view of the Roman Catholic *Magisterium*, we have reached the stage in which it is possible for us to proclaim an exceptionless and unchangeable norm regarding this matter. As for the handing on of life to new persons, the same *Magisterium* is sure that we have reached the stage in which we can state exceptionless and unchangeable norms governing the ways in which this may be done, in spite of the fact that changes regarding this matter did take place in the past, and in spite of the fact that the basis from which the so-called traditional teaching grew was an unhealthy one.

The fact that so many of us believe, at least at a subconscious

level, that we know what all the basics are can obscure our vision
so much that we do not see the real root causes of disagreement
among moral theologians regarding, for instance, the two sets
of norms just mentioned. This point has been brought to the
fore in an article by Jean Porter in which she voices the opinion
that 'the current debate in Catholic moral theology concerning
the foundations of moral obligation might more fruitfully be
cast as a debate over rival accounts of the human good, than
as a debate over the moral significance of particular goods'.[15]
If such an approach had been taken a long time ago, without
real or supposed authorities and their mesmerizing influence
getting in the way, numerous errors in teaching might have
been avoided. For instance, the available evidence suggests that
it is simply not true that *nobody* was aware of the basic importance to humans of justice and friendship and that *nobody* was
sufficiently sensitive to the injustice and downright unfriend-
liness of slavery before the seventeenth or eighteenth century.
Much more than a thousand years earlier, Gregory of Nyssa
was able to write:

> 'I have owned slaves, both men and women.'
>
> You condemn a person to slavery whose nature is free and
> independent, and you make laws opposed to God and con-
> trary to His natural law. For you have subjected one who was
> made precisely to be lord of the earth, and whom the Creator
> intended to be a ruler, to the yoke of slavery, in resistance
> to and rejection of His divine precept. Have you forgotten
> what limits were given to your authority? . . .
>
> How is it . . . that you should act against a free nature,
> bringing down one who is of the same nature as yourself, to
> the level of fourfooted beasts or inferior creatures . . .? . . .
> But you have abused the nature of service and of ownership,
> and have made service into slavery for yourself and have
> obtained ownership over the owner.
>
> 'I have owned slaves, both men and women.'

Tell me, what price did you pay to acquire them? What is the equivalent in goods for the cost of human nature? How much, in terms of money, is the value of intelligence? What price did you pay, in obols, for the image of God? For how many staters did you buy a human nature made by God? . . . For One who has known human nature said that not even the whole world is a sufficient price for a just payment for the soul of a man . . .

Is there any difference in any respect between slave and master? . . . Do they not both preserve their nature by eating the same food? Is there not the same structure of internal organs? Do not both become the same dust after death? Do they not have the same judgment? Do they not go to the same heaven or the same hell? You who are equal in all respects, why should you be superior such that while you are only a man you think that you can be the owner of a man?[16]

There would seem to be grounds here for suspecting that Gregory's understanding of what we might call certain basic human goods did not coincide exactly with that of many, perhaps the majority, of his contemporaries or with that of innumerable scholars who came after him. Something similar can be said regarding the telling of untruths. We have already had reason to note hard-line attitudes expressed in the writings of Augustine and in the *Summa Fratris Alexandri*. Some softening seems to have entered into early twentieth-century manuals of moral theology. John Dedek notes that there we find a distinction being made between *falsiloquium* (commonly translated into English as 'falsehood') and *mendacium* (which is translated as 'lie'). What is more surprising is that Dedek found this distinction foreshadowed in the writings of Peter of Poitiers and St Albert the Great, although 'it never took hold or was developed in the medieval tradition',[17] and Peter himself did not consistently apply it.[18] Now, as we have already noted, for many present-day traditionalists and revisionists – perhaps the vast majority of those involved in the debate about proportionalism – truth is a basic human good. It would appear that Augustine would not have described it as such, but he and numerous other scholars of earlier centuries did regard it as something to be venerated, something that, according to the *Summa Fratris Alexandri* is more noble than life, something, it would seem, to which humans should bend the knee. It matters not that Augustine and possibly other writers of former times did not regard truth as a basic human good. The fact remains that, if they regarded truth as more noble than life, their vision of the human good differed from that of Grisez, Finnis and numerous other present-day scholars – both traditionalists and revisionists. It would also seem that there were significant differences between the 'hardliners' led by Augustine on the one hand and Albert and Peter on the other. If, then, there were disagreements among scholars in ancient times concerning what present-day scholars see to be aspects of the human good, and if there are clear disagreements concerning the same matter between present-day scholars and luminaries of former times, is it not possible that we will find something similar happening today among the participants of debates between traditionalists and revisionists?

Let us, then, try looking at the current debate between the proportionalists and the Grisez–Finnis school as one about different accounts of the human good. Remember that what we are dealing with at this level is the fullness of human being and those things that fulfil humans as persons. Now, a basic tenet of the Grisez–Finnis school of thought is that one should never turn directly against one of the human goods. We should not be moved by hostility, says Grisez, to choose or accept the destruction or impeding of any of these goods, and we should not be moved by a stronger desire for an instance of one of them to choose to act for it by destroying, damaging or impeding an instance of one of the other goods, because, by such choosing, we would determine ourselves against the good to be damaged, impeded or destroyed. Side effects which are contrary to one of the goods may, however, be accepted, because such acceptance does not amount to determining oneself against the good in question.[19] Even within Grisez's own scheme of things, however, things are not quite as simple as that, for, as we saw in Chapter 2, Grisez holds that Catholics should comply with the teachings of the *Magisterium* even when that teaching is in error, because God has not yet provided a better norm for their belief and practice.[20] We have also seen that one such error on the part of the *Magisterium* was Leo X's condemnation of Luther's statement that it is against the will of the Holy Spirit to burn heretics at the stake. Grisez, of course, accepts that this was an error on Leo's part. That, however, is not the problem. The problem is whether or not Catholics at that time should have complied with the Pope's teaching. It would seem that, in Grisez's opinion, they ought to have done so. If this means that a Catholic would have been wrong to refuse to burn a heretic or to express disapproval of such action, do we not have to conclude that a Catholic would have been right in turning against the good of life in such a case in favour of another good? Having discussed this and the problem of direct attacks on the good of justice and friendship that might have arisen out of the 1866 Holy Office Instruction regarding slavery, I concluded in a recently published article that, in Grisez's scheme of things, the moral rightness of actions is dependent upon the fulfilment of the basic human goods, '*except where such fulfilment would conflict with the will of God as expressed through the Magisterium of the Roman Catholic Church*'.[21] Such a teaching, of course, could only apply to Roman Catholics and would mean that a Catholic would be justified in turning directly against a certain human good in a certain way during one period in history, but not in another, depending upon the most recent papal pronouncement regarding the matter in question. Even if we disregard this complication, however, we find that, not only do the proportionalists disagree with Grisez regarding the attitude that Catholics should have towards the *Magisterium*, they also disagree that human fulfilment is necessarily damaged by choosing against one of the human goods in the ways described by Grisez. Although there are some differences among the proportionalists themselves, we can say that, in general, they hold that the moral rightness or wrongness of an action is to be determined by taking stock of all the various ontic goods and evils involved.[22] If, in a particular case, this process leads to a choice of an instance of one human good, rather than another, so be it. The limits of space, time and sin-filled situations in which we find ourselves make such choices inevitable.

It would appear that, among other things, two different ways of dealing with tradition are being displayed here. Grisez apparently believes that the Catholic *Magisterium* is the best available teacher and interpreter of tradition, in spite of the fact that it makes mistakes – even very serious ones – from time to time. Indeed, he holds that responsibly following the judgement of the *Magisterium* in a particular case, even though that judgement may be erroneous, is the same as responsibly and sincerely following one's conscience in other cases.[23] While respecting Grisez's opinion, many other scholars, I imagine, will find that very difficult to accept, if for no other reason than the fact that many people were aware of the erroneous status of various teachings of the *Magisterium* long before those teachings were changed for the better. Let the teachings on slavery, the burning of heretics and witches, and religious liberty suffice as examples.

In short, then, proportionalists, on the whole, do not entirely agree with Grisez on this matter. He, in turn, classifies them as dissenters and goes so far as to claim that most dissenting Catholic moral theologians are proportionalists.[24] What, however, can we say about the proportionalists' own attitude to tradition?

I said earlier that most revisionist moral theologians set great store on tradition. That is, in general, true of the proportionalists, and rightly so, I venture to suggest. However, there are indications that they have perhaps not always been as discerning regarding this matter as they might have been. Many, perhaps most, of them seem to have adopted the Grisez–Finnis notion of a list of basic human goods – or, if not that, something very similar to it. I am not suggesting that this notion is necessarily a mistaken one, but they might do well to ask themselves whether they are expressing a traditionalist tendency to stick 'constant and unchangeable' labels on things. There may be a problem, moreover, in a tendency to believe, at least at a subconscious level, that we know more or less all there is to know about what is involved in full human being. It seems to me that we would do better to openly declare our ignorance in this sphere, to acknowledge that we know a certain amount, and suspect a few other things, but that much more may come to light in the future.

Another problem associated with the basic human goods arises out of our way of dealing with them. Grisez and Russell Shaw state clearly that they do not claim that those goods have an independent existence like Platonic Ideas.[25] It seems to me, however, that they are often treated rather like Platonic Ideas by members of both schools of thought, including, some might wish to add, the author of the present work, in earlier writings. This too would seem to be the result of inadequate discernment concerning traditional teachings on Christian ethics. The tendency to treat goods as something similar to Plato's Ideas is clearly shown in some ancient writings. Talking about truth as being more noble than life is one indication of it. Are we to demand that human persons should bend the knee to the Idea of truth, or are we to seek the fulfilment of persons? Surely the latter, but claims that one should never intentionally deceive another person even to save somebody's life would seem to lean towards the former. Grisez, it is true, speaks about the human goods as aspects of persons, but references to turning against the goods and to their incommensurability can, and I think often do, lead to their being treated as separate entities. This

has complicated the whole discussion about the viability of proportionalism, for it is said that proportionalists call for comparison of goods, and that no such comparison is possible
because the goods have no common denominator. As far as I
am aware, no proportionalist so far has given a thoroughly satis-
fying response to this objection. It seems to me, however, that,
as long as we continue to treat these goods as if they were
separate entities, no such response is possible.

Since the early days of what has sometimes been referred to
as the marriage between Greek philosophy and Christianity,
there has been a tendency within the Church for scholars to try
to put concepts into neat little boxes. Such imaginary containers
can be useful. Problems arise, however, when we forget that
they are only imaginary and that the concepts concerned cannot
be so confined in reality. Thus we find ourselves forgetting that
the aspects of persons which are sometimes referred to as human
goods are not really distinct entities. What may be missed in
that last phrase is the full import of the adjective. If they are
all aspects of persons, the goods are not really all that distinct,
separate, independent. It may be useful, on occasions, to talk
about comparing goods or values, but I am not at all sure that,
when we are trying to find out what is best for human fulfilment
in particular cases, we are merely comparing values. Let me
give an example. Carl Jung tells us that, when he was writing
his book about the libido, and nearing the end of the chapter
entitled 'The Sacrifice', he knew in advance that its publication
would cost him his friendship with Sigmund Freud. He knew
that Freud would never be able to accept his ideas on the subject
of incest:

> I spoke with my wife about this, and told her of my fears.
> She attempted to reassure me, for she thought that Freud
> would magnanimously raise no objections, although he
> might not accept my views. I myself was convinced that he
> could not do so. For two months I was unable to touch my

pen, so tormented was I by the conflict. Should I keep my thoughts to myself, or should I risk the loss of so important a friendship? At last I resolved to go ahead with the writing – and it did indeed cost me Freud's friendship.[26]

Whatever one might think of Jung's ideas on incest, if one looked at the problem from his point of view, one might see it as involving a conflict between truth and friendship – a choice between imparting knowledge and preserving a friendship. Such a way of looking at things, however, can be quite misleading. From what Jung tells us, it seems that, in order to preserve his friendship with Freud, he would have had to pretend to accept the latter's ideas regarding incest. But surely a friend is someone who accepts me as I am, not as he or she would like me to be. There are lots of people who will accept me if I put on a mask for them and behave as they wish me to behave, but they are not my friends. If Jung had not published the book in question, he might have preserved a certain kind of acquaintanceship with Freud, but to what extent that relationship would have been a friendship, in the full sense of that word, is, to say the least, debatable. From the moment that Jung realized that their relationship depended upon his pretending to be what he was not, the friendship was in question. The upshot of all this, for our purposes, is that truth and friendship are not totally separate entities or even totally distinct aspects of persons. Friendship exists when two people *truly* accept and love each other, as they *truly* are, at least insofar as that is possible. To resolve the moral dilemma, then, we need not resort to value-balancing or worry about turning to one value and against another.

It will be remembered that one of the chief arguments advanced against proportionalism is that the various goods are incommensurable. They have, we are told, no common denominator. This would seem to mean that the viability of proportionalism is dependent upon our being able to apply mathematics to ethical problems. The case we have just discussed, however, shows that the mere fact that, according to certain theories, the values or goods of friendship and truth are incommensurable does not prove that proportionalism is unworkable. Assuming that the facts of this case were as stated, we can continue to say, if we like, that Jung had a proportionate reason for having his book published. The fact that, in resolving this case, we have not confined ourselves to mathematics or even pseudo-mathematics to demonstrate the proportion merely supports Edward Vacek's observation, made a few years ago, that we are more than mere computers that can only deal with data reducible to multiples of a common denominator.[27]

Once it is realized that we are not dealing with values which bear a striking resemblance to Platonic Ideas and which have an unfortunate habit of competing with each other for our affection, the mathematical problem is seen to be a red herring. Let us take as another example for analysis the much-discussed problem of telling an untruth about the whereabouts of his intended victim to a known assassin with the deliberate intention of misleading him. This is sometimes presented as a case involving a conflict between truth and life. Such thinking merely diverts us away from what is really happening. To tell the truth to the murderer would do no good to him or to the informant. It goes without saying that it would not do any good to the intended victim. On the other hand, preserving the life of the last mentioned by deceiving the assassin could, in normal circumstances, quite obviously be productive of good for all concerned. Once again, there is no need to resort to apparently impossible value-balancing.

This kind of analysis of cases of apparent conflict of values could be applied, perhaps less controversially, in the realm of social ethics when seeking to explain how to justify taking what belongs to another without that person's permission in cases of dire need. Let us suppose that a poor man has no food for himself or his family. They have not eaten for a considerable period of time, and the people who could help refuse to do so. He decides, therefore, to resort to what, in other circumstances, we might call stealing.[28] It is true that, in commenting upon the justifiability of the 'stealing' in such cases, some ethicists have been content to say that the right to life is more important than the right to property. In this case, however, we can get help in going beyond that by turning to teachings found in what are sometimes referred to as 'traditional writings' regarding the subject of ownership. A number of the Fathers of the Church, taking it as basic teaching that the goods of the earth are intended by God to be for the benefit of all people, pointed out that giving alms to the poor could be otherwise described as restoring to them what is rightfully theirs or even, in some cases, as restitution of stolen goods, although the goods in question, in a particular case, may have been acquired legally. Thus we find rich people who refuse to share what they have with the poor being described as bandits and savages.[29] Some of the Fathers did, of course, accept a limited notion of private ownership as stewardship. That much could also be said of Thomas Aquinas, who was of the opinion that private ownership was necessary for three reasons:

> First, because each person takes more trouble to care for something that is his sole responsibility than what is held in common or by many – for in such a case each individual shirks the work and leaves the responsibility to somebody else, which is what happens when too many officials are involved. Second, because human affairs are more efficiently organized if each person has his own responsibility to discharge; there would be chaos if everybody cared for everything. Third, because men live together in greater peace where everyone is content with his task. We do, in fact, notice that quarrels often break out amongst men who hold things in common without distinction.

The community of goods, he tells us, however, is a part of natural law. Private ownership is not a matter for natural law, but it is not contrary to natural law. It is a matter for human agreement and is what rational beings arrive at as an addition to natural law. He then goes on to take the discussion beyond the need to care for and distribute the resources of this world. There is also the question of how to use and manage them. We are not entitled to manage things merely for ourselves, he says. We should do so for the benefit of all, and thus be ready to share with others in case of necessity.[30] If, of course, one believes that material things have been created for the good of us all, it is easy for one to appreciate what has so far been said about the attitudes of both Aquinas and the Fathers. It is also easy to see that one would not be a good steward of what one owned if one did not give to the poor in times of dire necessity. When such is the case, when nobody is willing to share, poor people are left with no alternative than to take what should have been given. There is not really a clash here, then, between some independently existing value or Idea called 'the right to life' and another called 'the right to private property'. There is merely a clarification of what is involved in good stewardship, a reminder that one has goods for others as well as for oneself, and that those goods should be used in accordance with needs.

One difference between this case and the others I discussed above is that here we can more easily turn to tradition for support in our analysis. This, I venture to suggest, is partly because our inheritance regarding this matter is more developed than is our inheritance regarding various other ethical issues (some of which we have discussed in this book), and partly because traditional teaching on private ownership does not describe it as an absolute value or a basic good. If, however, we accept, as indeed I think we must, that there are no basic goods which exist as separate entities to which human beings must bow, there is nothing to prevent our using this kind of analysis in cases in which tradition has not led the way. As has already been noted, Grisez and others of his school claim that the basic goods are not separate from but are indeed intrinsic to persons. Things that are extrinsic to persons, they say, may be used for the good of persons, 'but what is intrinsic to persons has a kind of sacredness and may not be violated'. One must therefore remain open to all the goods. To do so is, according to this school of thought, to adopt an inclusivistic attitude. As one might expect, the attitude that any one basic good of persons may be violated directly to achieve another is described as exclusivistic. Exclusivistic choosing, furthermore, betrays a preference for some part or other. 'And since these goods are not apart from persons, a selective love of goods is a selective love of persons.'[31] This sounds impressive, but the fact remains that telling the truth to an assassin about the whereabouts of his proposed victim does not promote the human good – in the sense of what is really good for humans. Telling an untruth in such circumstances would not necessarily involve selective love. Furthermore, one would surely not be displaying equal love for assassin and victim, and anybody else who might be involved, by telling the truth. Indeed, freely choosing to tell the truth in such circumstances when knowing the probable consequences of such action might well indicate selective love, or at least a lack of love towards the proposed victim. To talk of truth as being part of or an aspect of the persons involved in such cases makes no more sense, it seems to me, than to talk of private ownership as part of the persons involved in the case involving taking what another has without that person's permission because of dire need.

Robert P. George recently commented on an article of mine, referred to above,[32] in which I discussed, among other things, problems arising from treating truth and other such concepts as Ideas towards which humans should bend the knee:

In fact, Hoose's guess that Grisez and Finnis would ground an absolute prohibition of lying on the good of truth is only partly correct. In chapter seven of the soon-to-be-published second volume of his masterwork, *The Way of the Lord Jesus* ('Living a Christian Life'), Grisez argues that the exceptionless norm against lying is grounded mainly on other goods; and, as it happens, he provides a complex argument to show that it would be wrong to lie even to protect someone from being murdered. The nerve of his argument is not the value (abstract or otherwise) of truth, but, rather, primarily the self-alienation (which is opposed to the goods of self-integration and authenticity) that is involved in any choice to lie.

This changes nothing in my basic argument. If the basic goods of self-integration and authenticity are treated as distinct entities, they present the same sort of problems that the 'Idea' of truth presents. It can, of course, be claimed that any person telling an untruth will necessarily become less self-integrated and less authentic, but what grounds do we have for claiming that? Grisez describes self-integration as harmony among all the parts of a person that can be engaged in freely chosen action, while authenticity is 'harmony among moral reflection, free choices, and their execution'.[33] I fail to see how any lack of such harmonies would necessarily come about in a person as a result of telling an untruth to a serial killer, for example, about the whereabouts of his or her next intended victim. If we say that it does, it would seem that we should also say the same about using violence to protect the would-be victim, in spite of the fact that traditionalists, including Grisez, would permit such an action where it is necessary. In fact, Grisez says that killing a person in such a case 'may be accepted as a side effect of the use of the minimum adequate defensive force, provided one acts both fairly and mercifully in accepting it', and provided the death is not intended as an end or chosen as a means.[34] Many would, no doubt, want to debate with him on that matter. In my argument, however, I have not referred to killing. I am merely talking about the use of violence. It seems that the basic good (or 'Idea') of truth is always made a special case.

This, continues George, does not mean that one must reveal the whereabouts of a potential victim to a would-be murderer. He declares, wrongly as it happens, that I had assumed that there are only two possibilities in such a case:

> (1) to lie or (2) to provide the homicidal maniac with the information he demands. He [Hoose] omits three other possibilities, all of which Grisez mentions: (3) to remain silent, (4) to say something true and appropriate in the situation while avoiding giving the killer the information he wants, and (5) to do something to divert the questioner or prevent him from causing the prospective harm.

It seems clear to George that Grisez would hold that the first two options may not be legitimately chosen, 'for one is under obligations *both* not to lie *and* not to reveal to the maniac the whereabouts of the potential victim'. One must, therefore, choose from among the other options.[35]

Such argument as this reminds one of the verbal and mental gymnastics to which many sincere Catholics in Britain and Ireland apparently felt themselves obliged to resort in penal times when striving not to reveal the whereabouts of priests. One is also reminded of the enormous problems associated with such restrictions on choice. Let us take (3) above, the first of the three options which are acceptable to George – and presumably to Grisez. The experience of many people down through the centuries has shown us that, in certain kinds of situations, remaining silent proclaims the truth just as loudly as speaking it. As for the option (4), I remember a case which I was told about some years ago. I shall invent a name for the person sought because I do not recall the real one. Some soldiers arrived at a house and knocked at the door. A tall, slim man opened up. 'Is Albert Bloggs here?' asked the officer in charge of the soldiers. 'I think he is just about to go out', replied the tall man. At that the soldiers rushed into the house, and the tall, slim man, who was Albert Bloggs, ran off down the road while the soldiers searched his house. We could say that this man said something which was true and appropriate in the situation while avoiding giving the soldiers the information they wanted. The problem is that such solutions are available only to the very quick-witted, and even they could be expected to run short of ideas on occasions. Similar problems are found when we try appealing to (5), the third of the 'acceptable' options. The fact is that what George says merely serves to underline what I have said above regarding the widespread call to bend the knee to truth and other goods.

In the book to which George refers, and which has since been published, Grisez writes:

> But even someone certain he or she was speaking with a person intent on committing murder would not be acting as love requires if, judging that person to be beyond repentance, he or she resorted to lying in an effort to save the potential victim's life. Rather, treating as neighbors both the potential victim and the enemy would require not giving the information and, usually, explaining why: 'I will not answer your question and help you do wrong; instead, for your soul's sake, I ask you to repent of your wicked intent.' Such an answer might or might not succeed, but it is a work of hope, while lying is an act of desperation.[36]

It goes without saying that a person who resorts to telling an untruth in such circumstances is not necessarily judging the recipient of the misinformation to be beyond repentance. As for the final sentence, we could just as well say that addressing a man about to kill a child with the words 'Please do not do that because it is wicked' is an act of hope, while hitting him is an act of desperation. Most people would probably agree, but would still regard such a violent act as morally justifiable if the situation were desperate. So too, I imagine, would most 'traditionalist' moral theologians. We are left, then, with the problem of Ideas like truth, self-integration, authenticity and all that I have said above in that regard.

It is surprising that, in recent debate, so much emphasis has been laid on the incommensurability of goods or values. After all, the need for a proportionate reason has been a part of Christian ethics for so long that many people might be inclined to call it traditional. Even the principle of double effect includes as one of its conditions the need for a proportionate reason for bringing about the evil effect. The mere fact of that evil effect's resulting indirectly does not suffice. The principle of the lesser evil and the principle of totality also leave to the agent the job of working out proportion. Any break with that requirement, which is apparently what some 'traditionalists' are calling for, could, therefore, be quite reasonably described as a break with tradition. The mere idea of breaking with tradition on a particular point is not all that shocking, but one would expect it to be identified as such by traditionalists. Moreover, what we have seen in the Jung case, and in the others that we have analysed, does not lead us to suppose that a complete break is necessary or advisable, although it does seem that there are reasons for modifications regarding what should be involved in seeking proportion. What we need to break with, it seems to me, is the tendency to think of goods or values as, at best, distinct aspects, and, at worst, separate entities. It may also be the case that labelling certain things as good always and everywhere is misleading. Take, for instance, the case of deceiving a known serial killer about the whereabouts of his next intended victim. What could possibly be good about telling him the truth? If truth were indeed a separate entity, a Platonic Idea or a god to which humans must always bend the knee, there might at least be a case for consistently referring to it as good, but, as it is none of those things, I am not sure that even referring to it as an ontic good in such a case serves any purpose other than that of bringing about another apparent conflict – between truth and life. If we are concerned principally with human fulfilment, surely we have to say in this case that deceiving the killer is obviously the best way to promote it. Even if we wish to talk about what is good for the killer, and not just for the victim and the person doing the deceiving, we surely cannot believe that the killer will somehow benefit in some mysterious way from being the recipient of a truthful statement about his proposed victim's whereabouts. Surely, if he is going to be impressed or otherwise positively affected by anything, he will be so affected by the love shown through the action of the protective deceiver.

In short, although it may not be easy to analyse all cases in a way similar to that employed for Jung's dilemma regarding his relationship with Freud, it seems to me that such analysis does help us to see that talk about incommensurability of goods or values is misleading. Given our present state of knowledge, it may well be that the best we can do in certain cases is to describe and analyse them in terms of values. This will not necessarily be a problem if we do not treat those values as separate entities. Such an approach does not satisfy us intellectually, because we cannot always explain clearly how we come to a certain conclusion. It seems to me, however, that this problem arises from our ignorance about what it is to be fully human and/or a certain lack of analysis of much of which we are unthematically aware. Attempting to analyse our sensitivities can only lead to improvement in the situation. The histories of slavery and religious liberty have surely indicated that much.

Undoubtedly, we have much to learn from past teachers, but, when our moral sensitivities and analysis of those sensitivities warn us that certain aspects of what we have inherited may be part of that unwisdom referred to by Kelly, we should not shrink from the task of seeking the wisdom that eluded our forebears. Now, it seems to me that the tendency to treat goods or values as more or less separate entities, while perhaps not being fully aware of the fact that they were doing so, was not among the wisest things that some of our more influential forebears did, and it also seems to me that we would do well to move away from that way of thinking. This could prove to be a very difficult task, but, it seems to me, a worthwhile one.

NOTES

1. Kevin T. Kelly, *New Directions in Moral Theology: The Challenge of Being Human* (London: Geoffrey Chapman, 1992), p. 2.
2. Ibid. Kelly is referring more specifically to Roman Catholic tradition, but notes that there is a shadow side to tradition within the human family as a whole.
3. Germain Grisez, *Christian Moral Principles*, vol. 1 of *The Way of The Lord Jesus* (Chicago: Franciscan Herald Press, 1983), p. 121.
4. The list of goods presented here is an abbreviated version of that presented in: Germain Grisez, John Finnis and Joseph Boyle, 'Practical principles, moral truth and ultimate ends', *The American Journal of Jurisprudence* 32 (1987), pp. 107f.
5. Grisez, *Christian Moral Principles*, pp. 127–8.
6. Ibid., pp. 807–8.
7. Etienne Gilson, *The Christian Philosophy of Saint Augustine* (London: Victor Gollancz, 1961), pp. 4–7.
8. John F. Dedek, 'Intrinsically evil acts: An historical study of the mind of St Thomas', *The Thomist* 43 (1979), p. 400.
9. Germain Grisez and Russell Shaw, *Beyond the New Morality: The Responsibilities of Freedom* (Notre Dame: University of Notre Dame Press, 1980), pp. 74–5.
10. John M. Finnis, 'Natural law and unnatural acts', *Heythrop Journal* 11 (1970), p. 375.
11. Grisez, *Christian Moral Reasoning*, p. 902.
12. Grisez and John C. Ford discuss this report in their article 'Contraception and the infallibility of the ordinary Magisterium', *Theological Studies* 39 (1978), pp. 258–312.
13. W. F. Hogan writes: 'Many theologians attribute infallible teaching authority to the syllabus itself, while others deny this. Nevertheless, the syllabus must be accepted by all Catholics, since it comes from the Pope as universal teacher and judge, according to the official communication from Cardinal Antonelli accompanying it. Its contents cannot be challenged by Catholics, and they are to give assent to it, holding the

opposite of the condemned propositions' ('Syllabus of Errors' in *New Catholic Encyclopedia* (New York: McGraw-Hill, 1967), p. 855.

14. Pius IX, *Syllabus* 77 and 78.

15. Jean Porter, 'Basic goods and the human good in recent Catholic moral theology', *The Thomist* 57 (1993), pp. 27–8.

16. *Fourth Homily on Ecclesiastes*: PG 44, 665f.; translation as in J. F. Maxwell, *Slavery and the Catholic Church* (London: Barry Rose Publishers, 1975), p. 33. Some present-day moral theologians may disagree with some of what Gregory has to say (some of which I have omitted) about animals in this passage.

17. Dedek, 'Intrinsically evil acts', p. 412.

18. John F. Dedek, 'Moral absolutes in the predecessors of St Thomas', *Theological Studies* 38 (1977), p. 680.

19. Grisez, *Christian Moral Principles*, pp. 226 and 240.

20. See Chapter 2, note 8.

21. B. Hoose, 'Proportionalists, deontologists and the human good', *Heythrop Journal* 33 (1992), p. 184.

22. The terms 'ontic good' and 'ontic evil' are used by many contemporary authors to express what was more commonly meant by 'physical good' and 'physical evil' in older writings. Some authors replace 'ontic' with 'premoral' or 'nonmoral'. Some years ago, Louis Janssens explained ontic evil as 'any lack of a perfection at which we aim, any lack of fulfilment which frustrates our natural urges and makes us suffer' ('Ontic evil and moral evil' in *Readings in Moral Theology* No. 1: *Moral Norms and Catholic Tradition*, ed. C. E. Curran and R. A. McCormick (New York: Paulist Press, 1979), p. 60.

23. Grisez, *Christian Moral Principles*, p. 884.

24. Ibid., p. 11.

25. Grisez and Shaw, *Beyond the New Morality*, p. 71.

26. C. G. Jung, *Memories, Dreams, Reflections* (London: Fontana, 1977), p. 191.

27. Edward Vacek, 'Proportionalism: one view of the debate', *Theological Studies* 46 (1985), p. 304. John Finnis recently commented that the present writer 'absurdly persists in claiming that proportionalists reach their conclusions by "calculations"'. My 'central confusion', he went on to add, 'is to suppose that if any comparisons of value (e.g., human beings are more valuable than stones) can be made, it must be possible to make proportionalist comparisons of the premoral goods and bads involved in *options* for morally significant choice. *Non sequitur*' (*Moral Absolutes: Tradition, Revision and Truth* (Washington DC: The Catholic University of America Press, 1991), p. 100, n. 38). Such words as 'calculate' and 'work out' have a mathematical ring to them. That is unfortunate, and I certainly did not intend to indicate in my earlier writings on proportionalism, to which Finnis refers, that calculations in the strict mathematical sense were involved. That, I thought, was

clearly stated. I hope that the examples given in this chapter will suffice to show precisely how the determination of rightness and wrongness is, or at least can be, effected. I imagine, however, that some people will continue to loosely employ words like 'calculations', 'calculate' and 'work out' even when making analyses such as those found in this chapter.

28. 'Stealing' is one of those words which some writers have described as containing a moral condemnation. They would stress that, in the case under discussion, we are merely talking about taking the property of another person without that person's permission.

29. For a deeper discussion of the attitude of the Fathers, see William J. Walsh and John P. Langan, 'Patristic social consciousness – The Church and the poor', in *The Faith That Does Justice: Examining the Christian Sources for Social Change*, ed. John C. Haughey (New York: Paulist Press, 1977), pp. 113–51.

30. *Summa theologiae* IIa IIae, 66, 2. Translation Marcus Lefébure (London: Blackfriars, 1975).

31. See Grisez and Shaw, *Beyond the New Morality*, p. 141.

32. See Chapter 2, note 8.

33. Grisez, *Christian Moral Principles*, p. 124.

34. Germain Grisez, *The Way of the Lord Jesus*, vol. 2: *Living a Christian Life* (Quincy, Illinois: Franciscan Press, 1993), pp. 483–4.

35. Robert P. George, 'Liberty under the moral law: B. Hoose's critique of the Grisez–Finnis theory of human good', *Heythrop Journal* 34 (1993), p. 177.

36. Grisez, *Living a Christian Life*, pp. 406–7.

Index